STUDIES OF TYPE-IMAGES
IN POETRY, RELIGION,
AND PHILOSOPHY

STUDIES
OF TYPE-IMAGES

IN POETRY, RELIGION,
AND PHILOSOPHY

By

MAUD BODKIN

Geoffrey Cumberlege

OXFORD UNIVERSITY PRESS

LONDON   NEW YORK   TORONTO

1951

Oxford University Press, Amen House, London, E.C. 4

GLASGOW   NEW YORK   TORONTO   MELBOURNE   WELLINGTON
BOMBAY   CALCUTTA   MADRAS   CAPE TOWN

Geoffrey Cumberlege, Publisher to the University

Printed in Great Britain by
A Brown & Sons, Ltd., Hull

PREFACE

'OF these studies—or essays, as from their freely ranging character they might have been entitled—a friend wrote to me: 'the important questions dealt with need considerably longer treatment'. I have been keenly conscious of the need not for greater length of treatment with my present resources, but for wider, more intimate knowledge than is within my power of history and world-literature in its whole range. Then the presence in human experience of those patterns I have termed archetypal, and the way they appear in varying imagery evolved by different races of men could, I believe, be more convincingly demonstrated.

Yet, realizing my inadequacy, I found that I must make the attempt to carry further what I had essayed to do in *Archetypal Patterns in Poetry*. If in the writing and reading of poetry such patterns and images are operative, equally they must be present in those religious and philosophic writings not named as poetry where men express their vision or theory of human capacity and the human condition, its origin and meaning. For those of us who cannot accept the dogmas of any religion as uniquely revealed by God, faith may be possible that the more universal ideas or patterns underlying these doctrines are God-given, their evolution into greater clarity and relevance to life part of the divine intention for man. In this faith the attempt, inadequate as it may be, to trace such patterns in world-literature and relate them to present need becomes part of our duty to God.

· M.B.

1950.

ACKNOWLEDGEMENTS

I owe thanks to the many authors whose work I have used; also acknowledgements to those owners of copyright who have given me permission to make quotations: Messrs. Wm. Heinemann Ltd. for quotations from *Flight to Arras* by Saint-Exupéry; to Messrs. Faber & Faber for quotations from the poetry of T. S. Eliot and of W. H. Auden; to Messrs. Curtis Brown Ltd. for lines from *The Ascent of F.6* by W. H. Auden and Christopher Isherwood; to Messrs. J. M. Dent & Sons Ltd. for sentences translated by F. M. Cornford in *Greek Religious Thought*; to Phoenix House for a passage from the *Bhagavad-Gita* translated by Swami Prabhavananda and Christopher Isherwood; to Messrs. George Allen & Unwin Ltd. for a passage from *The First Europe* by Delisle Burns; to the Hogarth Press for lines from *A Time to Dance* by C. Day Lewis; and to the Clarendon Press, Oxford, for quotations from *The Greek Commonwealth* by Sir Alfred Zimmern and from *Four Stages of Greek Religion* by Gilbert Murray. The following poems or extracts from the works of W. B. Yeats are used by permission of Messrs. Macmillan & Co. Ltd. (London), Messrs. A. P. Watt & Son, and The Macmillan Company, New York (owners of the American Copyright): 'The Second Coming' from *Later Poems*, 1924; extracts from 'Sailing to Byzantium', 'Meditation in Time of Civil War', 'Nineteen Hundred and Nineteen', 'Prayer for My Son' from *The Tower*, 1928; and from 'The Countess Cathleen', *Poetical Works*, 1907, 1935.

ANALYTICAL TABLE OF CONTENTS

PREFACE   *v*

ACKNOWLEDGEMENTS   *vi*

I. IMAGES AND EXPERIENCE OF GOD

I. The intention of this essay is to consider, with reference to their validity, the diverse images of God through which men seek to attain and express experience of God, encounter with Him. Since reflection on such a theme is inevitably influenced by the individual history and resources of the thinker, some indication is given of the writer's spiritual history. Among directive influences were the writings of Plato, Albert Schweitzer, C. J. Jung.   *page 1*

II. In the study, by recent methods of psychological analysis, of poetic and religious tradition, there appeared two main types of imagery of the Divine. They may be termed—following F. M. Cornford in his study of Greek religion—Dionysian and Olympian. In considering both types account is to be taken of the highest and completest as well as the earlier and cruder forms. The Dionysian pattern in its highest form is illumined by the New Testament records. A present-day illustration is found in Saint-Exupéry's *Flight to Arras*. The Olympian pattern in less developed form is illustrated from the Old Testament and from recent regressive manifestations; in its highest form from the writings of Plato and Dante.   *page 9*

III. We have need of religious images, yet the course of history gives little ground for confidence in the saving power of any archetype. Can we find any criterion for testing the different forms of religious imagery? If, accepting no absolute revelation, we yet dare to assume a Divine intention present in the process of evolution from a planet uninhabited, through forms of merely animal life to the world of man as known to-day, it is in man's distinctive attribute—Reason in its completest sense—that we must find the criterion for judgement of religious images; Reason held to include the power of recognizing the *I-Thou* relation.   *page 20*

IV. Martin Buber, writing of the *I-Thou* relation, regards it as possible within three spheres: that of our life with nature, with ideas, and with our fellow men—the relation being clearest where with our fellow men it is mutual. Where the relation is, through recorded words, with the spirit of one speaking to us from the past, we find a distinctive analogy for the relation with the Divine. Yet for complete encounter by creatures of flesh and spirit there is need that the body take part. On this need depends the value for some minds of external images. More essential is bodily participation in the relation to God through service of man, as suggested in the parable of the Last Judgement.   *page 24*

V. Using to focus our thought an instance of present-day service, we question what creative contribution to the idea presented in the parable comes from the experience and thought of our time. Psychological studies have quickened our sense of the complexity of those psycho-physical dispositions which provide motivation for the intentions of the spirit. The sense of guilt and of responsibility to our fellows may sometimes be psychologically explained, as regards its particular form, by reference to experiences of childhood, yet receives justification from deeper sources.   *page 28*

VI. The recognition by our reason of other centres of value and demand valid as our own, making us members of a spiritual order clashing with the animal order to which we also belong, justifies both our sense of guilt and the archetype of a suffering and atoning divinity immanent in man. This same recognition and clash suggests that the true image of God transcendent is of a being not omnipotent but infinite in wisdom and will for the redemption of a world whose perversity, both at human and sub-human levels, does not originate in him. Thus the action of God on the world—conceived according to Whitehead's formulation of his nature, primordial and consequent —may be thought under the image of the ideal statesman persuading men to the wisest course, in the interest of the whole, that their conflicting self-interests and limited outlooks suffer them to accept.   *page 32*

VII. Such a concept of the divine nature appears relevant in relation to our increasing awareness of the part-responsibility of every member of a community for its collective action. The religious thinker accepting this idea of the Divine may feel less bewilderment at the grievous record of the past and at present disaster, while he still seeks to discern, within the sphere of contemporary national and international action, that which seems nearest to the divine intention—understood as fulfilment of the potentialities of individuals in harmony with one another and with the forces sustaining their lives. To the present writer the Tennessee Valley experiment appears an instance of such action. *page 38*

VIII. Among problems of the individual religious life, prayer is considered as the spirit's quest for strength and enlightenment; in this quest archetypal images may have part. For many minds to-day rational scepticism excludes prayer for modification of external happenings; such scepticism, integrated into faith, may not exclude prayer for other spirits. *page 46*

IX. Faith in encounter with God in earthly life generates a hope for more adequate meeting after death. For the present writer that hope finds expression—against a background of expected re-incarnation—in imagery of a momentary sharing of the divine vision. *page 52*

X. Reviewing her intention in the present essay, the writer speaks of hope for a rebirth of religious faith, requiring essentially sincerity in individual expression with respect for differing expression in others. *page 57*

II. THE IMAGE OF THE DIVINE BIRTH

I. Yeats' poem, *The Second Coming*, is here taken as the starting point of a study of the image of divine, or numinous, birth. The poem, considered as addressing us in its own individuality, brings together in a new powerful whole, word-meanings—the birth at Bethlehem, the 'cradle' of the divine child, the 'Second Coming'—that have evocative power through a long history: these meanings to be con-sidered in relation to the image of the 'rough beast', and to present conditions. *page 63*

II. The earliest image known to us of divine birth is found in that pattern of myth and ritual characterizing the religions of ancient Egypt, Babylon and Canaan. The ritual symbolized, and was intended to promote, the rebirth of plant and animal life. In the

Orphic religion we find recognized need also for the rebirth of the soul. It has been argued that the emergence of the idea of the soul, or spirit, as immortal and divine is connected with the experience of intoxication or ecstasy, variously induced—an hypothesis in line with certain other experience, though perplexing to our feeling.

page 68

III. Valuing that image of the Divine Birth fashioned for us by the Gospel writers, and by artists of later ages, we may yet, for the necessities of our time, require another image, to which have contributed both historic research, and the metaphysical speculation of our own and other ages and peoples. In different stories of a divine power entering the world we find the pattern of a conflict to be waged between good and evil. Recent research into the relation between the recorded life and teaching of Jesus and the tradition he inherited illumines the form of this conflict in his thought—the Kingdom of God as an inbreaking sphere of power overcoming the Kingdom of Satan. The influence is shown also of the ancient pattern of the god who dies and rises to victory. In the thought-image of the birth and life of Jesus, shaped through such research, we may still recognize, as in the older image, a great type and instance of the union of human and divine. *page 73*

IV. In the writings of Nietzsche we may recognize the influence of the same Idea, or archetype, operative in Yeats' poem. In the Superman Nietzsche anticipated with desire a Birth embodying both the good and the evil he felt struggling within himself and the world. More aptly, however, in the imagery of Yeats' poem than in that of Nietzsche is conveyed the relation of these forces in human life. *page 87*

V. Passages of poetry are compared to illustrate the use and power of the image of divine birth. The birth of Jesus appears as a symbol of suffering and death, as well as of inbreaking life and light. In its wider ranges of meaning the symbol has relation to every creative moment of life and to every human birth. *page 95*

VI. In any poetic image that wins our deep response we may divine, and, at a venture, put into conceptual terms, an inner meaning interpretative of life. In Yeats' poem, *The Second Coming*, this central meaning to the present writer appears as the universal tragedy of our history: how the entry of the Divine into the world becomes obscured, even changed for a time into its opposite, through the influence of the element in which—as in resistant clay—it must be realized. Yet the divine thing, never vanquished utterly, rises anew.

page 104

III. THE SAGE, THE IMAGE OF WISDOM

I. The intention of this essay is to examine images of wisdom found in poetic and religious writings, from these images gathering some idea of the need that has shaped them—a need which may also be considered in its expression in human institutions. Chosen passages of poetry give preliminary indication of the type-image and the shaping need. *page 109*

II. The two figures most vividly presented in religious records, Jesus Christ and Gautama Buddha, are considered in their aspect as teaching and embodying a saving wisdom. The figure of the human Jesus, as identified in St. John's Gospel with the Divine wisdom, the Logos, is interpreted to us through our own historic tradition. The Buddha, as the numinous central figure of a religious tradition, is harder for us to interpret. In his recorded teaching the Buddha appears to express a wholly agnostic attitude to whatever lies beyond this life; but his relation to his immediate and later disciples suggests that his teaching communicated implicitly a positive element—a relation to a divine and eternal reality—such as other Eastern sages have made explicit. The wisdom taught and embodied by the great figures of religious records, which still wins response from us (the agreement of Jung, as medical psychologist, with the teaching of a Chinese sage is given as one example) witnesses to a persisting spiritual need. *pages 113*

III. The image of wisdom appears in the idealized figures of priest and king, as well as of prophet. The relation between these types is considered, especially that between priest and king, as illustrated in the conflict between Archbishop Becket and King Henry II. Taking as an image of wisdom the figure of Archbishop Becket, as it appears in religious record, and in T. S. Eliot's play, *Murder in the Cathedral*, we find both 'problem' and 'mystery', as Gabriel Marcel has distinguished these terms. With the problem of the image of wisdom embodied in a priestly figure we are concerned as we try to trace the causes of the reverence given to the priesthood in the middle ages. We encounter mystery when in the figure of priest, or of king, we recognize the presence of God to man. *page 125*

IV. The question is raised whether in our present-day society we can recognize a spiritual organization in which the same functions are fulfilled that in the past pertained to king, prophet, priest. To the ancient image of kingship we may relate the occasional experience in recent times of something numinous in the appearance of wise leadership—a leadership appearing more effectively, both to poets and to peoples, in war than in that way of peace now so necessary to our survival. *page 135*

V. Can we recognize in our present society figures corresponding to the priest and prophet of past times, embodying in some degree the spiritual aspect of wisdom? In considering this question we reject such sharp division between material and spiritual as Julien Benda makes, or P. A. Sorokin. If we can recognize in the imaginative and philosophic writers of to-day an order of 'clerks' still maintaining and furthering spiritual awareness, we find the focus of such awareness to be on completer encounter of each human spirit, as materially, historically conditioned, with others also thus conditioned. *page 147*

VI. If we think of the imaginative writers of to-day as shaping through individual vision and communicating to their readers images that are a growth of the time, though based on the ancient archetypes, we can understand why the image thus communicated of wisdom should be no more than a suggestion of the direction in which wisdom lies. The 'archetype'—indicated by Jung through various metaphors and approaches—is a term hard to define, because of the elusive, inter-penetrative, character of the psychic and spiritual life to which it applies. In its subjective aspect the archetype can be described as a psycho-physical disposition. Objectively it appears in images preserved through words and pictorial forms. Beyond this characterization, we may recognize the archetypes of Wisdom, and of the Divine birth, as communicated through the encounter of finite beings, and, through this, of finite with infinite spirit. *page 167*

INDEX : I.—Subjects. II.—Names. *page 181*

I

IMAGES AND EXPERIENCE

OF GOD

I

THE theme of this essay is the diversity of images or forms
through which men recall and express their experience of
the Divine: this in relation to the question of the reality of
that experience. The essay is written by one who maintains, though not easily, faith in the existence of God, and
is addressed especially to those who also maintain or desire
such faith, but are unable to accept the whole teaching of
the Christian Church.

I use the phrase 'experience of God', but the word
'experience' in this relation has been challenged by a writer
whose work has done much to illuminate religious consciousness in our time. In his book *Ich und Du*,[1] Martin Buber
has confined the term 'experience' (*erfahrung*) to the relation
of the *I*, the human person, with things, objects, feelings—
bounded existences. The relation of the human *I* with God
is not such an experience. It is a meeting with a *Thou*, a
being unbounded, known only through encounter, not to be
enclosed within any image or conceptual formula we may
use in trying to communicate that never wholly communicable meeting. Though I have ventured to use the word
'experience' in a sense wider than Buber allows, I agree with
his emphasis on the term 'encounter' (*Begegnung*). It suggests
more forcibly the contrast I wish to consider, between the
diverse images, objects or forms of thought, which men use
as vehicles of reference and means of approach to God, and

[1] Published 1923, translated by R. Gregor Smith, *I and Thou* (T. & T.
Clark, 1937).

that contact with reality beyond all images which it is the aim of religion to achieve.

We who live in a country nominally, or by tradition, Christian, especially the older among us, have been offered from our earlist days certain images and practices as pre-eminently fitted to mediate encounter with the Divine: the images presented in the Old and New Testaments, the practice of joining in some form of common worship. In relation to these images and practices, let us consider two recorded instances of individual religious experience.

'I cannot remember a time', writes John Baillie,[1] 'when I did not know that my parents and their household were part of a wider community which was under the same single authority'—that authority and Presence with which he found himself 'confronted' when he first heard stories from the Bible read or told. Wherever else in later life he experienced encounter with the Divine, 'it was', says Baillie, 'the same Presence as met me in the Bible'. 'All of the past through which I am addressed in the present is centred in the story of the Incarnation and the Cross.'[2]

In contrast with this, another instance. After telling, in her essay *Alpha and Omega*,[3] how she had reacted from her early 'Low Church' upbringing, first 'into rather extreme High Churchism' and then into agnosticism, Dr. Jane Harrison writes: 'Having tried all the theologies open to me I came to the conclusion that religion was not for me, that it said nothing to my spiritual life, and I threw myself passionately into the study of literature and art. . . . And then within my own professional work it happened rather oddly that I became slowly aware that what I really was interested in was, not Greek art, but Greek religion, and even Greek literature held me largely for its profoundly religious content.' And again, 'I owe [theology] a sort of

---

[1] *Our Knowledge of God* (Oxford University Press, 1939), p. 183.
[2] *ibid.* p. 86.   [3] *Alpha and Omega* (London, 1915), pp. 184-5.

grudge, because the impossibility of accepting its man-made figments made me for years think I was irreligious, whereas I know myself by temperament to be deeply, perhaps almost insanely, religious. The unseen is always haunting me, surging up behind the visible.'[1] In many passages of her writings Jane Harrison has indicated these unseen forces present in the manifestations of Greek and more primitive religion, and has communicated to responsive readers something of her own conviction that the approach to unseen reality which she studied in so many strange myths and rituals was a thing of immense significance, 'worth a lifetime's devotion'.[2]

These fragments of autobiography illustrate the diversity of form through which different individuals encounter the Divine: the failure of forms significant in one life to make any similar appeal to another. Also, I think any reader of these two authors must realize how much these brief passages of self-revelation contribute to the understanding of the ideas that elsewhere they more impersonally present. In following their argument we are helped to supply something of the presuppositions, the inner atmosphere, which the reader must imaginatively contribute in order adequately to share the thought, its implied rejections and exclusions, as well as what it explicitly asserts.

It is because I have again and again found a writer's ideas on moral and religious themes illuminated by some indication of his life history that I venture now to introduce what I wish to say concerning images and experience of God by some autobiographical reference to determining influences on my own thought. I speak first of encounter with the Gospel story and practices of Christian worship.

That story came to me read and told by my mother and nurse, by the minister of the Congregational Church we attended, and by his daughter who conducted a Bible class

[1] *op. cit.* p. 206. [2] *ibid.* p. 186.

for children of the congregation. My adolescent experience, like that of Jane Harrison, was of reaction against all the ideas of God and of the worship of God, conveyed to me through this early teaching. The agnostic attitude of my father had, no doubt, some influence on this reaction, particularly through the sense of disunity in family life. Yet no memory remains of any utterances of my father sceptical or critical of religion. I knew that he spent much of his time reading philosophical works, and that he wished that I too should study philosophy, yet when he talked, as he sometimes did at meal times, of the books he was reading, while we children sat round the table rather unwillingly detained, his talk seemed to waken in me as little response at that time as did the religious teaching of my mother. I could almost adopt, in application to my own experience, the words of George Tyrrell: 'as soon as ever I ceased merely to repeat the formulae of religion, and began to translate them into realities, the whole thing vanished as completely as Jack and the Beanstalk; not by reflex reason and negation, but because there seemed no object to lay hold of'.[1]

The imagery and forms offered me seemed utterly unreal, yet I was conscious of a need they were meant to meet and did not. I recall one Sunday evening when I sat in the Congregational Church—a dreary interior whose meagre, painted pillars supporting a heavy gallery had become for me a symbol of my own heavy boredom as I sat, a child staring at them, during long sermons. At this time, this evening I am recalling, I was not a child but adolescent— the daughter whose turn it was to accompany mother to the service. The minister was preaching from the text, *Behold I stand at the door and knock*, and the image was in my mind of Holman Hunt's 'Light of the World'. There swept over me a wondering impatience at the form, rigid and fantastic as

[1] *Autobiography of George Tyrrell*, arranged by M. D. Petre (Arnold, 1912) p. 69.

it seemed to me, in which was presented the offer of a secure happiness and peace I would have desired if I could have conceived a possibility of finding it. I knew no one whom I could believe had found it. My mother's troubled hold on the teaching and practices of her church had not brought her peace. My own earlier attempts at certain moments to respond to the pleading of evangelists conducting special missions had brought nothing but disappointment and revulsion. I thought—as Jane Harrison concluded after her youthful experiences—religion is not for me, says nothing to me.

At college the *Phaedo* of Plato was among the books set for reading in Greek. While I struggled with the language, the image formed slowly and took root in my mind of a man happy, secure and at peace in his death, through the power of philosophic thought. 'The lovers of wisdom know that philosophy receiving their soul plainly bound and glued to the body and compelled to view things through this, as through a prison . . . endeavours to free it. . . . The soul of the philosopher, therefore, thinking that she ought not to oppose this deliverance abstains as much as possible from pleasures and desires, griefs and fears . . . following the guidance of reason and being always intent on this, con-templating that which is true and divine and being nourished by it.'[1]

At college I was often unhappy, through shyness and diffidence in company with others. I knew what it was to feel the body a prison, and to long for some vision of a truth independent of all bodily and individual desire and frustra-tion. Could the study of philosophy bring one such a vision, such freedom?

I could say, with Simmias in the dialogue, 'It appears to me, as it probably does to you, Socrates, with respect to these matters, that to know them clearly in the present life

---

[1] *Phaedo*, 82-4.

B

is either impossible or very difficult.' Yet it seemed to me, as to him, that the possibility was worth testing with all one's resources, 'learning from others or discovering for oneself' something concerning the ultimate realities of life and death, 'taking the best of human reasonings and that which is the most difficult to be refuted and embarking on this, as one who risks himself on a raft, so to sail through life'.[1]

After the *Phaedo* I read many of the other dialogues of Plato, re-reading again and again especially that great passage in the *Phaedrus* that describes in myth the vision of divine truth: 'There are, it is true, many ravishing views and opening paths within the bounds of heaven, whereon the blessed gods go to and fro, each performing his proper work, followed by whoso can and will; for envy has no place in the celestial choir. But when they go to banquet and high festival, they journey by a steep way to the summit of the heavenly vault. . . . The souls which are called immortal, when they reach the height, pass outside and take their stand on the outer surface of heaven, and there its revolution carries them round and they behold the things that are without. Of this region above the heaven no earthly poet has sung, or ever shall sing worthily. But this is the likeness of it . . . here is the dwelling-place of that colourless, shapeless, intangible reality which is visible only to reason, the guide of the soul, and is the object of all true knowledge. The mind then of deity being fed by pure reason and knowledge, and that part in every soul that seeks its due inheritance, is glad to see after long time that which truly is, and by the light of truth is fostered and made to thrive.'[2]

That this suggestion of a goal for human striving came in the form of myth commended it the more to my mind in revolt against dogmatic assertion. The appeal was strong in Plato's dialogues of that quality I later found described

[1] *ibid.* 85. [2] *Phaedrus*, 247.

as 'the urbanity of Plato'.[1] 'We must remember', says Timaeus, in the dialogue called by his name, 'that I who speak, and you my judges, are but men, so that in these matters it befits us to accept a likely story and demand no more.' And again, in the *Sophist:* 'Perhaps they may be in a difficulty and if so there is a possibility that they may accept a suggestion of ours respecting the nature of essence.' 'Can we', says Whitehead, commenting on this passage, 'imagine Augustine urbanely approaching Pelagius with "a suggestion of ours respecting the nature of Grace"?'

In the *Phaedo* I rejoiced in the challenge of Socrates: 'if I appear to you to say anything true, assent to it, but if not oppose me with all your might, taking care that in my zeal I do not deceive both myself and you, and like a bee depart leaving my sting behind.' Here was no hint of the appeal to fear, the threat of damnation to fall on any finding themselves unable to assent. The Christian teaching I had known in childhood held such a threat, and seemed oblivious of the danger of the sting left behind.

Amongst my earliest memories I find this incident. I was in my crib in the night nursery. It was at a time when I suffered much from night terrors, taking shape sometimes as fear of Hell and its flaming tortures. On this night, horror so far overcame my habitual caution in approaching my elders that I called the nurse and questioned her: Would not the fires of Hell some time, at last, go out, when people had been punished enough? The nurse replied: Never, but if one loved Jesus one would not go there. In the morning, I seem to remember, the nurse re-opened the question of loving Jesus as security against Hell. But cheerful daylight had then extinguished the poignancy of fear. I regretted the night's indiscretion and took refuge in silence. That one should love in order to escape punishment seemed to me,

---

[1] By A. N. Whitehead in *Adventures of Ideas* (Cambridge University Press, 1933), p. 152.

even then, too blank an impossibility to be worth consideration. I think now that the association in infancy of the figure of Jesus with the fear of Hell had a benumbing influence on feeling that to some extent persisted even when my outlook was transformed by fuller understanding.

The first real growth of understanding of which I am aware in regard to the Gospel story came with the reading of Albert Schweitzer's *Quest of the Historical Jesus.*[1] I was by this time a lecturer in psychology at a Training College, and had read enough of Biblical criticism and theology to see the Christian religion in a different light from that of my adolescent revulsion. Yet it seemed that the figure of Jesus could not appear with any vividness to me until Schweitzer —as I felt—swept away a mist of false teaching obscuring the humanity of Jesus; and showed me, in place of that dim, haloed, unintelligible image presented to my childhood, a heroic human sufferer, speaking inevitably the speech of his time, using its forms of thought, but loyal utterly to his own vision of God and truth, challenging us to be loyal, as he was, to truth shaped by the needs and intellectual insight of our day.

The life of a training college lecturer does not allow much leisure for the quest of ultimate truth, for testing, as Simmias wished to do, the philosophic hypotheses by which one might navigate life as on a raft. It was not till I retired from teaching that I was able, with this aim, to give myself for some years to the study of literature and philosophy.

The years of teaching had led me towards somewhat more practical lines of thought than my earlier studies followed. The contact with Schweitzer's writings, the new approach to the spirit of Jesus, helped, I think, to quicken a social conscience which had already wakened. I had joined the Fabian Society almost with the same feeling with which one might join the fellowship of a church. My parents had died,

[1] Translated by W. Montgomery (London, 1910).

leaving me money enough to live, if I chose, devoting myself to study. It seemed, at first while I had strength to work and earn my living, necessary to do so, giving money merely inherited to aid efforts of others to deal more directly than I could with the misery of the world. I wanted the help of the Fabians in understanding how to meet that claim I recognized of the disinherited upon one's conscience. Yet I had not the natural gifts for social investigation or propagandist work; and later, as health declined, it seemed that the life of thought I desired was permissible to me.

I had been drawn to study the psychology of Freud and Jung—that of Jung especially, partly for its philosophic interest, partly with the hope that his teaching, applied with medical help to my own problems, might have some effect on those inhibitions that from childhood had hampered me in social contacts. No notable success in this respect was obtained from the analysis I underwent. Yet I found value in a closer acquaintance with the less conscious ranges of the mind.

The greatest gain was perhaps a fuller sense of the unexplored wealth of the heritage communicated through language and custom, influencing unawares all our conscious individual thought and action. A suggestion for the study of this material was conveyed through Jung's hypothesis of primordial images or archetypes—residua of racial experiences, he calls them—which are stirred in the unconscious depths of the mind by the presentation of poetic myth. I wrote my book, *Archetypal Patterns in Poetry* (Oxford University Press, 1934) to examine and illustrate this hypothesis.

II

The thought of the diverse imagery used by different individuals in approaching the Divine was much in my mind as I pondered questions concerning the archetypal image of God. It seemed that two main types of image could be distinguished, as one followed back to their beginnings religious ritual and literary tradition. In *From Religion to Philosophy* (Arnold, 1912) F. M. Cornford has described two different aspects of the Power worshipped as divine in Greek religion—aspects which it seemed could serve as starting point for a more general study of the images of God. These aspects are represented by the contrasted figures of Dionysus, the mystery God, and Zeus, the Olympian.[1] In Dionysus, with his ritual drama of death and rebirth, the temporal aspect of nature and human life finds expression. The characteristic rite is sacramental. Through contemplation of the enacted drama, or some more active participation in ritual death and rebirth, the worshippers seek communion with the God and with each other. The Olympian God represents the spatial aspect of nature. Zeus, the original sky-God, Poseidon, God of the sea, Hades, of the underworld, has each his province. When Zeus becomes supreme, he is ruler over a dominion in which 'vested interests', or spheres of influence, remain to other deities. The relation of Zeus to his worshippers is a more external one than that of the mystery God. He is the ruler and lawgiver whom men fear and obey as they obey an earthly king, or as a child reverences the authority of his father.

In considering the response of our own minds to representations of the Divine, it seemed to me that we could distinguish archetypal patterns corresponding to these two figures: the pattern of a world-ruler essentially 'other' than ourselves, and that of a suffering hero and Saviour with whose sufferings and triumph over death we have intimate communion. Of these archetypes that of the suffering hero is stirred in response to the story of Jesus, while that of the all-powerful law-giver and king responds to the Jehovah of the Old Testament.

[1] *op. cit.* p. 111.

Freudian theory, so far as concerned with religion, has concentrated on the image of the world-ruler, identifying it with the 'super ego' or 'introjected' image of the father. The tyrannical aspects of the image, its repressive effects, are dwelt on. Little attention is given to the experience communicated by the writings of St. Paul and St. John, of joy and freedom in union with Christ and in casting off the tyranny of the Law. Relevance to this experience can be found only in the archetype of rebirth, and that joyful union with the God of which we find hints in studying the mystery religions.

In my book I did not attempt to go beyond the psychological question of the images, or the dispositions inherited or acquired, that may be recognized in our response to poetic myth or religious teaching. I had been interested and impressed by the theory of Durkheim emphasizing the importance for the religious life of the relation between the individual and the group, even identifying that Power which the individual encounters in his religious life with the group, or the group's collective force and achievement. At the time of writing I guarded against putting forward this view as a complete account of religion. It seemed to me none the less a hypothesis valuable to the psychologist.

The line of study I was attempting to follow was obviously different from psychology as a branch of science, with emphasis on analysis, measurement, experiment. There is value also, it seemed to me, in a psychology historic rather than scientific, that seeks to trace the growth of ideas and institutions as revealed in records of what men did and felt from earliest to later times. Imaginative and hypothetical such psychological work must be. Identifications will be made differently according to the different outlooks of those interpreting the record. Consider (e.g.) the central mystery of the Christian religion.

We all, with open face beholding as in a glass [R.V. *with unveiled face reflecting as in a mirror*] *the glory of the Lord, are changed into the same image.* In these words of St. Paul, no one, says B. W. Bacon,[1] can fail to recognize the vernacular of the mystery religions, who has any familiarity with their ideas concerning redemption through 'assimilation to the nature of a dying and rising Saviour-god by gazing upon his image'. Do we in this undeniable parallelism recognize an identity of pattern due to common dispositions active in men's minds in earlier and later ages?

Among anthropologists, Dr. E. O. James, in his work on the origins of sacrifice, has perhaps most clearly recognized the unity of the sacrificial, or—as it may also be termed— the rebirth, pattern, within widely differing modes of realization. The Gospel writers, he observes, when they represent Christ as 'describing his sacrifice in terms of a surrendered life to be shared with his followers', show 'profound insight into the fundamental character' of this ritual pattern in its manifold forms.[2] In the ritual shedding of blood it is not the taking of life that is fundamental, but the giving of life to promote and preserve life and to establish union between the individual and the unseen forces that surround him.[3] Whether the participation of the individual in the rite of sacrifice be by a sacred meal, or by passionate contemplation of a sacred drama, the same essential element is the identification realized by the participant between his own life and that stronger life, mysteriously purifying and renewing itself, which pertains to the sacred object.

From a different standpoint, the essential character of the likeness between the Gospel mystery and that of pagan religions has been strenuously denied. Thus, Dr. H. A. A. Kennedy[4] protests 'there is no true analogy . . . between the New Testament idea of fellowship in the sufferings of Christ

[1] *Jesus and Paul* (Hodder & Stoughton, 1921), p. 75.
[2] *Origins of Sacrifice* (Murray, 1933), p. 178.   [3] *op. cit.* p. 33.
[4] *St. Paul and the Mystery Religions* (Hodder & Stoughton, 1913), p. 214.

and . . . ritual sympathy' with pagan gods; since a new moral attitude, the acceptance of an ideal of love and self-sacrificing devotion is the 'core of the experience' of union with Christ, and this is lacking in the ritual experience of primitive or pagan worshipper.

Clearly when the purpose of our inquiry leads us to stress the moral element in experience, we must feel difference predominate over likeness in these examples. In the figure of the mystery god, Dionysus, Osiris, Attis, or in the yet older symbol of the springing corn, we find no explicit moral significance. Yet those who accept as fundamental within the sacrificial pattern the relation, however obscurely felt, of the individual to the larger life that sustains him, can recognize this factor as lying at the root of all conscious moral development. Viewed thus the image of Christ yielding himself to death willingly, for love of mankind and to awaken in men the sense of loving unity with him and one another, gathers up and completes the meaning obscurely present in the image of the wheat, or royal victim, or animal that gave unwillingly its sacred life that the life of the community might be renewed.[1]

'The only light I, personally, can ever get on anything', writes Jane Harrison, 'is by tracing it back to its first known beginnings.'[2] This saying seems to represent also the attitude of psychologists of the Freudian school. It is not, I think, adequate. When we examine, as I am suggesting we should do, each the images to us most significant within our own religious experience, there is value in tracing them back to analogies in the distant past; but it is in their fullest development rather than the earliest that their true nature appears. The psychologist who has meditated on the mystery of growth knows that its intermediate stages cannot be adequately explained from its beginnings, but rather from

[1] Quoted with slight alteration from *Archetypal Patterns in Poetry*, pp. 284-6.
[2] *Alpha and Omega*, p. 64.

the completed form. Our own life with its aspirations cannot be explained by its completion, since 'we know not yet what we shall be'—in this space-time dimension or in some other—but by entering imaginatively experiences we recognize as more fully developed than our own—completing meanings and tendencies of which we were dimly aware—we may come to understand better both our own images and efforts, and those more primitive ones with which also we acknowledge relationship.

I have spoken of the supremely valuable records in the New Testament, illuminating all experiences, whether earlier or later, that have the sacrificial or rebirth pattern. It is of interest, I think, to consider this pattern also in some present-day instances.

In the New Testament records there is stress on the relation of each individual to a group united by a common love and allegiance: *We know that we have passed from death unto life because we love the brethren.* At the present time there are some who find in an existing Church such lifegiving fellowship. For those of us who fail to find it there, the need remains to realize in some form the fellowship that brings release from egoism into larger life.

In her essay, 'Unanimism and Conversion', Jane Harrison has spoken of a kind of conversion, or rebirth experience, as possible to the scholar through devotion to science, and through the co-operation with others necessary in the pursuit of scientific truth. The universality of science demands surrender of all bias and pride of individuality; the supplementing and completion of one individual's work by another's gives entry into a spiritual fellowship. She speaks of touching most nearly the secret of ' Unanimism '—of realized liberating fellowship with others—in moments when some contribution from another worker answered a difficult question that had baffled her own researches. In this joyful co-operation of intellect one may not know one's helper in

the flesh. 'Perhaps', she writes, 'it is better you should not—
the body might divide you'; 'the body is the means, the
vehicle, of seclusion, of individuality'.[1]

My own experience has been similar to this. Yet I recognize a lack here. The body need not be always and only an
instrument of division. This is the type of experience of the
secluded scholar—all the more perhaps if the scholar is also a
woman and unmated. To such a one, imaginatively sharing
with pity and fear in the tragedies of war, or stresses of other
conflict, may come the thought that in these sufferings some
may find compensation through a union, closer than she can
know, of body and spirit in comradeship and service.

Among records of war-time experience one of the most
outstanding interest is *Flight to Arras* by Antoine Saint-
Exupéry. Nothing could illustrate more perfectly, it seems
to me, than this record, an encounter with the Divine
experienced, as in primitive Dionysian worship, through the
medium of group-emotion and participation in sacrifice, yet
penetrated by intellectual and spiritual insight complete as
any obtainable in our time.

Saint-Exupéry tells of the revelation that came to him
during the reconnaissance flight he was ordered to undertake at the time of the defeat of France in 1940. Believing
the flight to be useless and expecting death, he set forth in
that blank despondent mood that can feel no significance in
action. Because he was a writer, he tells us, he was 'free to
leave Group 2-33 the day I no longer approved of what I
was ordered to do'. But even during blank 'intermittances
of the spirit', and in view of good reasons for avoiding what
seemed vain sacrifice, he knew that he would not leave.
The 'notion of looking on at life has always been hateful to
me. . . . In order to be I must participate. Nothing is
stronger than the community of feeling that goes through
me when I say "We of Group 2-33". The particles, the

[1] *Alpha and Omega*, pp. 44, 77-8.

fragments that we are, collect and possess meaning in the fact of the Group.' He describes how, after the crisis of the perilous journey, when he found himself, against expectation, still living—having known death so imminent as to seem already experienced—more than ever he was interwoven with his group. 'Each of us had risked his life in more or less the same fashion.' 'What we could offer up, we had sacrificed.' He had earned the right of full communion with the rest. 'We dwell in the rot of defeat. Yet I am filled with a solemn jubilation, as if I had just come from a sacrament.'

Unlike the exaltation of those participating in primitive group-rites, this sacramental sense of unity enlarges itself toward universality. 'Through my comrades I was woven into the whole of my country', and beyond France, into the civilization of which France is a part. 'Love is a seed; it has only to sprout and its roots spread far and wide.' As, looking backward through the earliest records, we find the seed—the buried and springing corn—made the symbol of rebirth for man, so for this airman of to-day the seed-image brings assurance. 'All was threatened yet despite this, I could not but feel in myself the serenity of victory. . . . There is but one victory that I know is sure, and that is the victory that is lodged in the energy of the seed.' 'The seed stored up is a kind of heritage received by one generation of wheat after another . . . my civilization . . . too springs from energy contained within a seed.' 'For centuries my civilization contemplated God in the person of man. . . . As the inheritor of God, my civilization founded the respect for Man present in every individual' . . . man 'higher than the individual. . . . Man the seed whence springs our victory.'[1]

In this full and passionate description of a present-day experience we have, I think, an illuminating example of the appearance at a higher level of a pattern traceable through

[1] The words quoted occur between pages 120 and 147 in *Flight to Arras* by Antoine de Saint-Exupéry (translated Galantiere. Heinemann, 1942).

earlier phases of human development. The record recalls
descriptions of primitive Dionysian ecstasy—states of exalted
group-feeling into which little thought entered. Yet here is
present not feeling only but thought, reason at its completest.
That exalted awareness as of a life boundless, immortal,
which could be felt when individuality was submerged in
the group-excitement of primitive and barbarous rites,
which, again, can be experienced by the soldier made one
with his comrades in frenzy of battle for a cause whether
good or bad, is experienced here in relation to a reality fully
conceived as universal, divine, the same that men through
past ages have reverenced and sought to know. Can such
completeness in the powers of personality brought to the
encounter serve as any guarantee that the meeting is indeed
with the Divine?

Before we consider this question further from the philosophic standpoint, we may compare briefly some earlier and
later forms of the Olympian image of God.

The Olympian God we have noted as distinguished from
the Dionysian by his otherness, his relatively external relation to his worshippers. From nature also, the cycle of
death and rebirth, he stands apart. His relation to his
worshippers is that of ruler, lawgiver.

Professor Cornford has indicated the changes in the Greek
conception of Zeus, so far as these can be traced in surviving
literature. From his status as ruler of one province of the
world, subject to a mightier power, *Moira*, Destiny, Zeus
became himself 'dispenser of fate and upholder of the system
of provinces'. The power first attributed to impersonal
destiny, 're-interpreted into terms of human passion', appears
as jealousy ($\phi\theta\acute{o}\nu o\varsigma$) or *nemesis*, over against human presumption ($\H{\upsilon}\beta\rho\iota\varsigma$). 'Greek morality of the Olympian type',
Cornford observes, is governed by the precept to know
yourself and 'not go too far'.[1]

[1] *From Religion to Philosophy*, especially Ch. I, sections 6-13, and III, 69.

In the Jehovah of the Pentateuch we recognize the same character. The jealousy of God is a recurring motive; jealousy of honour paid to other gods, jealousy against man's presumption, his forbidden aspiration—according to the myths of Genesis—to divine knowledge and power.

Beside inheriting the repressive force of Destiny, the Olympian God has something of the character of the warrior chief. Zeus is 'the patriarchal God of the invading North-men', the Achaioi, 'who swept down on the Aegean kingdoms in the dawn of Greek history'.[1] Jehovah of the Old Testament, similarly, is at first the patriarchal God of an invading tribe, one whose prowess in war constituted a yet greater part of his character than did warlike energies in the representations left to us of the Greek Zeus. 'The Lord is a man of war. . . . Thy right hand, O Lord, is become glorious in power. Thy right hand, O Lord, has dashed in pieces the enemy.'[2] Many familiar passages in the Old Testament remind us of the form assumed among a warlike people by the image of God as king and leader. Within our own distinctive national tradition we recognize this image: Kipling's God, for instance, 'of the far flung battle line, Beneath whose awful hand we hold dominion . . . .'

In the Europe of our time the image of the divine war-leader has made a terrible reappearance. The deification of Hitler within the Nazi movement has shown how readily, in our day as in earlier times, a human leader can take on himself the projected archetype—appear endowed with super-human power, the *mana* or collective force of tribe or nation.[3]

The possibility, made vivid to us, of such deification compels us to realize the sinister aspect of the Olympian

---

[1] *Four Stages of Greek Religion* by Gilbert Murray (Oxford University Press, 1912), pp. 58, 68.

[2] Exodus XV, 36.

[3] Of the somewhat similar deification of Lenin and of Stalin, Professor Maynard has given illustration in his book, *The Russian Peasant* (Gollancz, 1942). Of Stalin, Maynard writes, 'he is hope and strength and guidance on the dangerous and difficult paths from oppression to freedom and

type-image. When God is worshipped as transcending man in power rather than in goodness, it would seem that through the worship forces devilish rather than divine may be encountered. There is, however, another character of the Olympian God which has had far-reaching effects of a different kind in the development of the archetype.

Zeus, the sky-god, is identified with 'the all seeing sun' coursing through the heavens. As humanized deity he has his home on the mountain top whence he looks down on the toilsome lives of men. The God of the ancient Hebrews similarly looked down from the heights of Mount Sinai on the idolatries of his people; and the imagery of our own worship still bids us look upward to God who 'from his throne beholds all the dwellers upon earth'.

The thought of a wider field of sight and knowledge, in quality akin but in range and organization far exceeding that of man, has special significance in the philosophic approach to the Divine. Plato and Dante alike make use of imagery of ascent, and of the imaginatively realized system of the circling heavens, to communicate an experience of vision wide-ranging and exalted beyond anything possible to the senses of man. In aspiration sharing with Deity that universal vision, the philosopher sees the troubles of his earthly life diminished and transformed. 'With my sight I turned', says Dante, 'back through all and every of the seven spheres, and saw this globe such that I smiled at its sorry semblance.' 'Do you think', says Plato, 'that a spirit

---

happiness'. He quotes from a poem published in *Pravda*, November 1937, lines referring to Stalin:

> *But one man there is on earth*
> *He is our path, our reason, our conscience.*
>
> . . . . .
>
> *The truth of the plain folk lived and lives in him.*

These words suggest the Christ image, God immanent rather than transcendent. Yet so far as the human leader is also thought of as remote, dealing with problems far beyond the simple citizen's power or understanding, the attitude falls under the Olympian pattern; the two forms interpenetrate.

privileged to contemplate all time and all existence can possibly attach any great importance to this life?'

An earthly ruler—a Caesar Augustus—lacking god-like powers of vision, yet needing the god-like survey over human affairs, had recourse to a system of news-bringing messengers. Similarly, the Book of Job tells of the day when the Sons of God, and Satan among them, came from going to and fro on the earth to present themselves before the Lord. From Zeus, also, according to Hesiod, went forth 'thrice ten thousand ministers' to keep watch over men's deeds of justice and unkindness.[1]

This image of the service of messengers, the contribution of individuals from their assigned different posts, as well as the image of world-wide vision has passed into the philosopher's concept of God. God, says Ortega y Gasset, has the use of all our perspectives.[2] God, says Whitehead, 'shares with every new creation its actual world'.[3] From the most dim and remote corners of the living universe may come a distinctive offering:

> The toad beneath the harrow knows
> Exactly where each tooth-point goes.

The intimate knowledge that is also suffering or enjoyment, possessed by each of us at every moment, we conceive as entering the awareness of God, a contribution toward that knowledge that is no mere external vision, or intellectual grasp, but a suffering with the creature known, an infinite compassion.

III

Let us at this point consider the outcome of this brief account of type-images of God. The few examples touched

---

[1] Hesiod: *Works and Days*, 225.
[2] *The Modern Theme* (translated by J. Clough. London, 1931), p. 95.
[3] *Process and Reality* (Cambridge University Press, 1929), p. 488.

on can, of course, illustrate little of that detailed diversity which is found when we attempt to enter imaginatively the religious experience of different individuals. The brief survey may, however, suggest something of the contrast present between the experiences we have termed higher and lower forms of the same archetype, and thus lead up to our question concerning the varied religious experiences of individuals. Do we believe that through them there can be encounter with a Divine reality?

Those of us who maintain faith that such a reality exists and does in some manner challenge and sustain us, can yet hardly escape misgiving when we contemplate the disastrous forms assumed by religion through the ages. The Christian religion, for all the commanding beauty of its presentation in the Gospel story and in passages of St. Paul's letters, falls in its subsequent history under the same judgement as other religious embodiments of archetypal images. The image of Christ on earth living and dying for man's salvation, the image of God, omnipotent Creator, Judge and Father of mankind—images each in some fashion accepted as objects of worship by millions of men—have not, it seems as we read human history, saved the worshippers from depths of evil, horrors of mutual destruction. Such a study as that by Aldous Huxley of Father Joseph, the Capuchin friar, *Grey Eminence*,[1] offers us an almost terrifying instance of the evil that may be accomplished through the life of one dedicated, as he believed, to the service of God, guided and strengthened by daily prayer and ecstatic contemplation of the passion of Christ. Whether we survey the operation of religious archetypes in primitive Dionysian orgies, priestly holocausts of victims animal or human, tortures and massacres in the name of the Christian God, or those perpetrated in our own time by Nazis inspired by the God of their Berserk ancestors,

---

[1] *Grey Eminence, A Study in Religion and Politics*, by Aldous Huxley (Chatto & Windus, 1941).

c

we have little reason to trust the power of men's images of the Divine to spiritualize and redeem their lives.

Nevertheless, the conviction remains that we cannot do without religious images. Both individually and socially our lives need the support of images, whether of more sensuous or conceptualized character, expressing our relations to unseen reality and to our fellow beings on earth. At the present time, when the structure of all our institutions and ways of life has suffered such shock and ruin, our minds turn the more anxiously to question what can sustain the values left to us, or aid renewal of those lost.

The importance of archetypal images, and of the commanding[1] experiences based on them, has been discussed recently from the sociological standpoint. Professor K. Mannheim in *Diagnosis of our Time*[2] has written of 'the disintegration of modern life-experience and conduct' caused by the disappearance or weakening of religious archetypes, no longer brought home to us, as once they were, in current literature and ceremonial observance. From the point of view of the sociologist, the function of the archetype recognized in common by a group or community is to extend and deepen the experience shared by the members with one another. Such shared experience, both emotional and volitional, should, it is suggested, precede and help to direct the more analytic experience concerned with ways and means which it is the function of science to develop.

The power of the archetype to rouse and direct the energies of men has also been emphasized, with reference to recent experience, by Arthur Koestler in *The Yogi and the Commissar*. The Fascists, he suggests, recognized this power and used it more effectively than did those 'of the Left' who

[1] The term used by Prof. Mannheim is 'paradeigmatic', for those basic experiences which are felt to reveal the meaning of life as a whole. I have preferred, as more directly significant, the term 'commanding', proposed by Dr. Oldham in writing of Mannheim's thesis.

[2] London, Kegan Paul, 1943.

worked for human freedom. Hoping to persuade through rational enlightenment, those called 'the intellectuals' forgot the really influential part of man, 'the subconscious, the older half of the brain, the archetype'.

If we accept this estimate of the power and necessity of archetypal images, yet recognize their frequently disastrous operation in human history, by what criterion can we distinguish between their different forms, judge whether through them we encounter a reality devilish or divine?

Let us examine somewhat further the notion of encounter with reality.

Our discussion of religious images as higher and lower, more and less developed, has dared to assume that in the process of evolution there is meaning—something we can regard as divine intention, values recognizable by our reason, present more fully in later than in earlier stages of the process.

This belief, or assumption, we should, I think, distinguish from the idea of 'progress' that took shape in the Victorian era, linked with an over-valuation—as now appears—of intellectual and material achievement. Whether the changes of the last century have or have not brought men nearer to fulfilment of divine intention is another question from that of whether we can recognize such intention in the evolution from an earth uninhabited, or by the primeval beasts only, to the world we know to-day—a civilization through all its conflicts yet lighted by the historic achievement of lawgivers, poets, saints, philosophers.

In the earliest attempts at reflection on the distinction between man and beast, the term Reason was used for man's distinctive attribute, and this Reason has been felt to be in some manner a link between man and God, the element within man's animal nature that reached out towards the Divine. There have been periods in which the idea of reason has narrowed, and the term suggested only a faculty of

using general ideas in the service of instinct and feeling.
But in our time philosophic reflection seems again moving
towards a wider view of man's distinctive attribute. Reason
must include, present-day philosophers have urged, whatever
power we possess of knowing ourselves and others as persons,
subjects, conscious communicating beings.

It seems to me, as Dr. Baillie has observed, that the
're-opening of the question of our knowledge of one another
is one of the most hopeful events in the philosophy of our
time'.[1] The essay by Martin Buber to which I have already
referred has helped to focus attention on this problem, the
question of all that is involved in the *I-Thou* relation. The
response to Buber's thesis, and the efforts of other contemporary thinkers to deal with the question in their own
terms, seem to show its relevance to our present need.

'In each *Thou*', says Buber, 'we address the eternal *Thou*.'
'God', says John Macmurray, 'is not primarily apprehended
as an idea, but in life which is centred in the intention of
mutuality, as that infinite person in which our finite human
relationships have their ground and their being.'[2] These
sayings seem to me to give a clue to our problem—to the
understanding of that encounter with the Divine which has
become possible to man through the process of evolution
from the beasts, and thought of which may help us to distinguish, among different forms of the type-imagery of God,
those at this point of the word's history valid for ourselves.

What then is the nature of this *I-Thou* relation, this
meeting with one another which may be also meeting with
God?

IV

In Buber's thought the full relation between man and
man is the complete form of a relation of which the human

---

[1] *Our Knowledge of God*, p. 201.
[2] *The Structure of Religious Experience* (Faber, 1936), p. 81.

spirit is capable 'through each process of becoming that is present to us'.[1] When I address a human being as *Thou*, and he responds to me, I am aware of our relation as mutual. Reflection on that mutuality shows me each of us in the encounter as *Thou* to the other, each in himself centering a universe—within a finite individuality, infinite. I do not first know myself and reflect on the mystery of my conscious being, then by analogy infer such consciousness in others. First in the history of the race and of the individual, through the beginnings of intercourse, comes dim awareness of mutuality, then growing consciousness of the *I* and *Thou* in mutual relation.

In 'the sphere of our life with nature' there is no such mutuality. Yet there is meeting. We may encounter a tree, a mountain, in such a manner that it is for us in some sense a *Thou*. In such encounter I with my whole being meet the tree in its completeness, not merely its serviceability to my purpose, its outward appearance or discoverable structure, but all of these and 'its intercourse with the elements and the stars', 'all present in a single whole'. Known thus, the tree also is a fellow being, a centre of relationship within a world.

With Ideas also—'intelligible forms' (*geistigen Wesenheiten*) shaping principles, not shaped counters, of thought—the *I-Thou* relation, in Buber's view, is possible. By such an Idea a man is challenged and responds with service. Buber speaks of the artist 'faced by a form which desires to be made through him into a work', 'demands' of him 'effective power'.[2] Challenged by such an Idea the scientist responds with long labour of observation and experiment; the philosopher builds his system of interlocking concepts.

Buber does not speak of that distinctive relation with ideas which appears to belong also to 'our life with men',

[1] *I and Thou*, p. 101.
[2] *op. cit.* p. 9.

when the idea by which the thinker is confronted is realized by him as communicated by another mind. When I become aware through the recorded words of Jesus, or Paul, or Plato, of some idea new to me, demanding to be realized in my life, is this a relation of mutuality? When Plato spoke or wrote, he meant his words to challenge every human spirit they could reach, whether at the moment of speaking or at any future time. In the response of my spirit to this intention it seems there is a certain mutuality, even though I cannot in my turn address and challenge Plato. In this sense at least, we can acknowledge as true what so many have felt burningly of the words of Jesus, that they live, challenging each of us, and through our response mutual relation comes to be.

In this type of relation between a human mind in the present and a voice—a spirit and intention—speaking disembodied from the past, there seems a special relevance to our problem. The realized mutual relation between the individual believer and the spirit of Christ—revealed through his words and through those of St. Paul and others adding their thought and intention to his—constitutes, it seems to me, the very centre of Christianity. Such living voices from the past, winning response and allegiance, offer perhaps a clue whereby the individual may test images and practices coming to him through institutional religion—through church and state and family. This would seem to be the distinctive faith of Protestantism, when the protestant impulse is carried to its conclusion, and dropping its hold on the letter of the Holy Book, dares to rely on the spirit addressing each individual conscience and reason.

Yet because we are creatures not of spirit only but of flesh, no relation can be complete for us unless the body has its share. Protestant teachers, impatient of the abuses of the Catholic sacramental system, and this Church's use of material images, have tended to ignore the need for some sensuous embodiment of spiritual grace. Those of us constrained to forego the support of either the Catholic or any Protestant Church have at least this compensation, that we are more free in thought to value whatever each Church has contributed to the civilization that surrounds it.

Thus we may at this point consider with sympathy the use in devotion, by Catholic believers, of images in that material sense we have so far disregarded—such images as the crucifix or the painted figures of Virgin and Child. Here is the archetype brought home to the mind through mediation of the bodily senses. Though we ourselves feel no need of such images—may find puritan austerity a more congenial setting for devotion—we can recognize as a greater error even than over-concentration on the symbol, that intolerance of another's need for symbolism that found historic expression in the fury of puritan image-breakers.

Personally I recall as illuminating the experience communicated in seeing some years ago the play by Sierra, *The Two Shepherds*. There is presented the old priest of a Spanish village, wisely and patiently ministering to his childish, turbulent flock; cherishing meanwhile a shabby ancient image of the Virgin and Child, which in quiet moments his lips address, while his spirit communes with the Presence—to him maternal in aspect—that supports him amid thankless labours. Such an instance may recall that 'defence of idols' for which Maximus of Tyre found words of memorable beauty: 'God Himself, the father and fashioner of all that is, older than the sun or sky, greater than time and eternity and all the flow of being, is unnameable by any lawgiver, unutterable by any voice, not to be seen by any eye. But we, being unable to apprehend His essence, use the help of sounds and names and pictures . . . yearning for the knowledge of Him, and in our weakness naming all that is beautiful in this world after His nature. . . . Why should I further examine and pass judgement about Images? . . . If a Greek is stirred to the remembrance of God by the art of Pheidias, an Egyptian by paying worship to animals, another man by a river, another by fire—I have no anger for their divergences; only let them know, let them love, let them remember.'[1]

Yet after fullest recognition of the need for tolerance and for sympathy in respect of human divergences, our need remains also for a criterion. Our reason must judge concerning more or less adequate means for making relation with the Divine *Thou*, so far beyond powers of sense and speech. We may find help in the thought of that other aspect of our bodily nature where it is not sensuously receptive merely but active.

In the earliest Christian teaching the parable of the Last Judgement gives expression to that requirement of 'works' of which Lutheran protestantism, with its emphasis on faith, failed to take adequate account. In the parable God is shown as making the service of man the essential means of relation with Himself: *Inasmuch as ye did it unto one of the least of these my brethren, ye did it to me.* The converse also: *Depart from me, ye who did it not*: relation with God denied where such service is lacking. The necessity of 'works'— helpful relation to the human *Thou*, as means of relation to God—could not be more forcibly presented.

v

If we accept, or entertain, this idea of relation to God dependent on relation of service to man, we may go on to question how this relation appears when translated from its simplicity of presentation in the parable into terms more closely relevant to our outlook and complex responsibilities to-day. It has been said[2] of Christian truth transmitted in

[1] Quoted in *Four Stages of Greek Religion* by Gilbert Murray (Oxford University Press, 1912), p. 98.
[2] By Professor Mannheim in *Diagnosis of Our Time*, p. 117.

parables—concrete images that do not so much define as 'point in the direction where Right is to be sought'—that scope is thus left 'for creative contribution in every new epoch'. What creative contribution can the thought of our own time make to the idea of relationship to God through service to man, as expressed in the parable?

Such contribution is, I think, possible from the whole range of research and philosophic reflection on the nature of man and society, set in the material and spiritual universe. What slight indication of all this can be attempted here may be introduced by an illustration from our own time, of direct service to man realized as relation to God.

In Albert Schweitzer's *On the Edge of the Primeval Forest*, and in his *Autobiography*, he has told how it became necessary to him to abandon the satisfactions of an academic career and go as a medical missionary to Africa. He has written of difficulties and discouragements experienced in his medical work, but has described also hours that were felt to compensate for all discouragements, when, through fellowship with the human creatures whose suffering he relieved, he is aware of fellowship also with the Divine. 'Because I am here', he writes, 'and am supplied by my friends with the necessary means' men can be saved from such torturing death as follows, for instance, an unhelped case of strangulated hernia. When such a sufferer, waking after operation, feels the relief of 'no more pain', he and others with him in the room may listen to words concerning 'the Lord Jesus who told the doctor and his wife to come to the Ogowe', and black and white together know by experience the meaning of the words 'and all ye are brethren'.[1]

Behind the simple language in which Schweitzer describes this hour of communion, is a consciousness penetrated by the thought and conflicts characteristic of our time.

[1] *On the Edge of the Primeval Forest* (translated Campion. Black, London. 1923), p. 93.

Consider his description of the impulse that brought him into his mission work.

In *Memoirs of Childhood and Youth* Schweitzer tells how he was haunted by thought of 'the misery which weighs so heavily upon the world', and the feeling that of this misery 'we must all take our share'. Sometimes this thought, 'left me alone so that I breathed freely again' but it had risen like a little cloud upon the horizon, and at last it 'hid the whole sky'. Under this oppression it seemed to him that the parable of Dives and Lazarus had been 'spoken directly of us'—of us Europeans, that is, who have innumerable means of fighting disease and pain, while 'out there in the colonies sits wretched Lazarus', 'the coloured folk', who suffer ills with no means of fighting them. As Dives sinned for want of thought of the poor man at his gate, so do we.[1]

In the light of psycho-analytic studies what should we think of this oppressive sense of guilt? Should we explain it in Freudian terms as connected with some misadventure in childhood—some revolt and hostile wish perhaps against a parent, rationalizing itself as a sin against humanity? It is possible that the peculiarly obsessive character of Schweitzer's concern for human suffering might have some such connexion. Certainly present-day awareness of such influences penetrating our conscientious convictions should make us examine these in the fullest light of rational reflection possible to us. Schweitzer's autobiography gives indication of such self-questioning, consideration from different points of view of his own physical and mental fitness for the work he had chosen. Yet in facing the remonstrances of friends against his intended course, it was not rational reflection but the sense of a divine call that was to him ultimate justification.

It seems to me necessary, in order to use rightly the resources psychologists have put at our disposal, that we

[1] *On the Edge of the Primeval Forest*, p. 1.

should distinguish two types of question, that concerned with psychological causes and that of ultimate moral justification. Professor Macmurray has suggested[1] that we might use the terms 'motivation' and 'intention' to distinguish, in regard to human behaviour, 'the proper field of scientific psychology' from that unobservable region where occur the ultimate choices of the spirit. The intentional action in which such choices take effect is conditioned, but not, we believe, wholly determined, by motivation resulting from all the habits established in the organism through the course of individual and ancestral history.

The relation of these two aspects of action, psychological motivation and intention of the spirit, has been illustrated vividly in a novel, *Arrival and Departure*, by Arthur Koestler. The book's chief character, member of a resistance movement, exhibits under questioning by torture a blind heroism. Having escaped his tormentors he suffers distressing after-effects for relief of which he has recourse to psychological analysis, and is shown 'the hidden roots of his action', the part played in his heroic resistance by his conditioning through early experiences. The conduct he had felt as heroic appears to him, in the first light of these explorations, futile, quixotic. Yet when he has planned to escape to safety from his course of life as identified with the struggling and oppressed, he finds he cannot. Deciding to continue to act in accordance with his intention before the disillusion of his analysis, he feels 'a peace which seemed to emanate from a source beyond [the analyst's] reach, from the very core of his self. She could prove that all his reasons were wrong; but perhaps in these spheres the right thing had always to be done for the wrong reasons. . . . Perhaps there were times when the source of that emanation, finding all outlets blocked, had to force its way through twisted and dubious channels to assert itself.'

[1] *The Boundaries of Science* (Faber, 1939), Ch. vi.

This saying seems to me to characterize aptly the relation between the 'intention' of the spirit and the 'motivation' of the organism through which the spirit must act. Twisted and dubious indeed may be the channels which the individual organism—the psycho-physical dispositions fashioned through past happenings—offers for the spirit's response to the influence theologians term the Grace of God, and which we may name the Divine Reason meeting the kindred element in man. Those who can maintain faith that God uses outward circumstances, however untoward, as means of communication with the human spirit, will not be daunted by thought of the twisted channels offered for that communication by the inner dispositions of the mind.

VI

There is more to be said concerning the problem of taming to the uses of the spirit recalcitrant energies of the body, and of the contribution of present-day thought toward understanding of the service through which men to-day may meet with God. But before considering further these questions we may revert to the problem already touched on in the suggestion of powers devilish rather than divine, possibly to be encountered through religious images. In the world of our experience we cannot assume equivalence between meeting with reality and with the Divine. The God we desire to know and to meet through service is good, but if good, can He also be all-pervading, omnipotent?

Let us look again at our instance of the recorded experience of Albert Schweitzer in his self-dedication to missionary service.

'Who can describe', Schweitzer writes, 'the injustice and the cruelties that in the course of centuries [the coloured races] have suffered at the hands of Europeans? Who can measure the misery produced among them by the fiery drinks and the hideous diseases that we have taken to them. . . . We and our civilization are burdened by a great debt. . . . Anything we can give them is not benevolence but atonement!'[1]

If, with Schweitzer, we recognize this debt, this need for atonement, incurred by a society that has inflicted such cruelties, what of those other cruelties inflicted, beyond range of any human responsibility, throughout the whole order of nature? Only a relatively small part of the diseases and sufferings of primitive people, and of others, can be traced to human sin. The preying of living organisms on one another is older than human depravity. No perversity of free-will in man can account for all the cruelty of life's devices at the sub-human level and within the instinctive, unconscious part of human life. What is the relation of the cruel conflicts we perceive throughout the whole world of creatures to our faith in a loving Creator?

Schweitzer's reaction to this problem is to turn from it as insoluble. We cannot comprehend 'the course of world events as the expression of a rational, ethical world will'. Yet the principle of 'Reverence for Life brings us into a spiritual relation with the world which is independent of all knowledge of the Universe'.[2] Through this principle we may find peace in accomplishing the service our individual position and resources make possible, feeling less the oppression of evil while we labour in fellowship towards its mitigation.

Schweitzer's principle of reverence for life, which to him came as a revelation after long perplexity, seems essentially the same as Buber's thesis that God may be encountered through every true *I-Thou* relationship. 'Only in the thinking man', says Schweitzer, 'has the Will-to-live become conscious' of itself—of the value of life with its possibilities of

[1] *On the Edge of the Primeval Forest*, p. 172.
[2] Albert Schweitzer: *My Life and Thought, an Autobiography* (translated Campion. Allen & Unwin, 1933), pp. 234-5.

development, in oneself and in other centres. The solidarity with other will-to-live desired in this realization cannot, however, be completely achieved 'because man is subject to the puzzling and terrible law of having to live at the cost of other life'. Here is the statement in Schweitzer's terms of the clash between the *I-Thou* relation possible to the spirit that recognizes other centres of needs valid as its own, and that type of relation to others, self-centred, predatory, in which through our animal nature we are all involved. In this clash within the thinking man of spiritual and animal nature would seem to lie the deepest origin of the sense of guilt with which Schweitzer and others have found themselves burdened. It was this same clash, subjection of the intention of the spirit to the law of the flesh, that wrung from St. Paul the cry: *Who shall deliver me from the body of this death?* St. Paul proclaimed deliverance through identification with the indwelling Christ, lover of all life, and through acceptance in that fellowship of a share in atoning suffering. Those of us who, with Schweitzer and Buber, have faith that we encounter God through the relation of human fellowship and service, recognize similarly by this test the validity of the archetype of the suffering God immanent in man. But what of that other archetypal image, of God the world-ruler—that archetype that, with loss of universality, takes shape so readily as a national or tribal tyrant-deity, or if conceived as truly universal, yet leaves us baffled by appearance of divine complicity in all the world's evil?

Though one may agree with Schweitzer that there is relief in abandoning any pretence to solution of the problem of evil and the suffering of the innocent, yet one may continue to desire some image, some working concept, of God transcendent that shall not involve contradiction so flagrant as to drain the life from faith. If I cannot believe in a God both loving and omnipotent creator of the world I know, yet I may find faith possible in a God whose love, wisdom, and power to redeem evil he did not create, transcends anything achieved or imagined by man. Such a God is imaged in Plato's myth of the Divine Reason that in the beginning 'took over' a flux, a chaos, 'moving without order or harmony', and, 'over-ruling necessity, persuaded her' towards order, the best that was possible.[1]

Professor Whitehead, marvelling at the degree to which Plato has anticipated through 'philosophic depth' of speculation the discoveries of modern thought, connects Plato's image as an 'allegory' with his own evolutionary doctrine of the emergence of different types of order, characterizing successive cosmic epochs.[2] In Whitehead's view God is the creator of the world, not as its First Cause, 'because our notion of causation concerns the relations of states of things within the actual world', but as the transcendent source of those forms of order without which no world could come to be. God is to be thought of as an agency not of compulsion 'omnipotently disposing a wholly derivative world', but of persuasion bringing some degree of harmony, 'aesthetic consistency', into a world whose other constituent of formless flux, 'creativity', does not originate in him.[3]

There is much in Whitehead's system, and in his account within that system of the nature of God, that is beyond the grasp of the writer of this essay; yet his development of Plato's idea of an agency of rational persuasion, operative through the whole universe with its different 'layers of types of order', appears to me a conception valid in relation to the archetype of God transcendent—one that each of us may realize as in some manner implicated in our experience, and may try to render explicit by help of traditional modes of representation.

[1] *Timaeus*, 29, 47.
[2] *Process and Reality* (Cambridge University Press, 1929), pp. 129-34.
[3] *Adventures of Ideas* (Cambridge University Press, 1933), p. 213. *Religion in the Making* (Cambridge University Press, 1930), p. 86. *Process and Reality*, p. 42.

We have considered the way in which the idea of the
Divine wisdom has taken imaginative shape within the
literary tradition as vision—such vision of the existing world
as we might conceive ourselves with vastly heightened
powers attaining, stationed on or beyond the circling
spheres; or again vision not of the transient actual but of
the eternal essences, such as, in Plato's myth, the Gods
enjoy, or souls before they fall into earthly bondage. These
two traditionally conceived types of vision Whitehead appro-
priates as aspects of God's nature postulated within his
philosophic system. The vision—or, as he prefers to term it,
the envisagement—of eternal essences, is the 'primordial
nature of God'[1]—that factor whereby within the universe
'there is importance, value and ideal beyond the actual'.[2]
The other aspect, 'God's consequent nature', is his awareness of each successive phase of the evolving universe, not
distantly—as in our image of extended sensuous vision—but
intimately of every minutest pulsation. 'He shares with
every new creation its actual world.'[3]

'The good which every soul pursues as the end of all its
actions, divining its existence, but perplexed and unable to
apprehend satisfactorily its nature'—this good conceived by
Plato, the central idea of that 'morality of aspiration' he
introduced into human thought—appears in Whitehead's
system as the primordial nature of God.[4] When, surveying
the society I know, I value it as embodying an aspiration
towards good—the inter-related good of all its members—
yet condemn it as betraying the ideal it embodies with such
manifold imperfection, that ideal, beyond the actual, by
which I judge, is not—so Plato and Whitehead maintain—a

[1] *Process and Reality*, pp. 44-6.
[2] *Modes of Thought* (Cambridge, 1938), p. 140 cf. *Religion in the Making*, p. 138.
[3] *Process and Reality*, p. 488.
[4] Every possibility of 'definiteness' is included by Whitehead within God's
primordial nature. That these possibilities are, however, ordered, graded
according to the essential goodness of the divine nature, appears to warrant
this relating of Whitehead's view to Plato's.

mere modification of my consciousness. It is a reality which, in Plato's image, lights my reason as the sun my bodily sight. In language used by Whitehead, this ideal by which I both value and condemn the world belongs to my 'sense of Deity', of transcendent worth beyond yet relevant to 'the multiplicity of realized actualities' encountered in my sensuous experience.[1]

Plato found it hard to indicate a relation between the intelligible forms, the unchanging real, which the soul finds kindred to herself, and that region of the changeable into which the bodily senses drag her—the sphere of that 'which is always becoming and perishing but never really is'. The thought of Plato's time, Whitehead suggests, had been 'dazzled by the glimpse of eternity' offered to it in the fundamental notions of mathematics. The 'static absolute' which the science of mathematics appeared to present 'passed over to philosophic theology as a primary pre-supposition—yet the great thinkers from whom we derive inspiration enjoyed insights beyond their own system'.[2] Such an insight was Plato's tentatively proposed definition of being as power—power to affect, or be affected by, another being.[3] The notion of Deity which, according to Whitehead, we find in 'human experience as shared by civilized intercourse', recognizes in God power both to act upon the changing world known to our senses and to receive reaction from that world. God's primordial nature—the eternal essences ordered in the divine envisagement in accordance with the divine goodness—acts persuasively upon the world, so far as 'physical agencies'—the world's already realized nature and the ultimate irrationality of its freedom —admit such action.

That resultant at any instant of physical agencies and the divine persuasion, entering the divine awareness—God's

---

[1] *Modes of Thought*, p. 140.　　　　[2] *Modes of Thought*, pp. 111, 113.
[3] *Adventures of Ideas*, Ch. V, 2.

D

consequent nature—is thought of as providing the new field of divine action, persuasive, redemptive. God's rôle—described by Whitehead as 'the patient operation of the overpowering rationality of his conceptual harmonization'—thus suggests the image of the ideal statesman persuading men to the wisest course in the interest of the whole that their conflicting self-interests and limited outlooks suffer them to accept.

VII

This conceptual representation by Whitehead of the divine nature in its two-fold character—unchanging, eternal, yet temporal in interaction with the changing world—though it presents difficulties such as can hardly be avoided in any human conception of the Divine, yet seems to me to have value and a distinctive relation to types of experience important to us to-day. I think especially of that experience, already illustrated from Schweitzer's writings, of responsibility felt by the individual for collective action—that of the state, or other collective whole, in which he has membership.

The call to meet God through service to man, which for those who first listened to Christian teaching could be adequately presented in terms of direct ministry to individual needs, takes on for us an aspect more complex and baffling. Those who first heard the words of Jesus, and those who formed the early Christian groups under the Roman Empire, had no responsibility for the government under which they lived. With the conditions necessary for its preservation and efficiency they were unconcerned.[1] On later ages the task has devolved of attempting to apply the ethical intuitions of Jesus to a society responsible for its own economic and political conditions, and inter-related with other such societies throughout the world. The idea of democracy

[1] Cf. Whitehead, *Adventures of Ideas*, p. 20.

which has come to mean so much to us, requires that even the humblest citizen should have some understanding of the acts of statesmen done in his name; while yet these acts involve responsibilities and demand resources of wisdom beyond the powers even of the most gifted and experienced individuals.

In a letter to Manning, having reference to the Land Bill of 1870, Gladstone wrote: 'I feel as if the happiness of some millions of God's creatures were immediately committed to us, so far as the things of this life (and their influence on another) are concerned; and until it is disposed of, it seems to engross and swallow up my whole personal existence.'[1] Like Schweitzer, Gladstone was troubled by a sense of guilt and need for atonement because of wrongs collectively committed—committed especially against Ireland. An undertone of remorse in him, in regard to the Government's repressive measures against Ireland, was, Hammond notes, recognized by his colleagues with scant sympathy.

Such anxiety and remorse on the part of a great statesman comes home with poignancy to those of us who to-day, even from our status of political insignificance, feel at times our personal existence 'swallowed up' in painful awareness of the suffering of millions in devastated Europe.[2] Thoughts arise seeking escape from this oppression: 'What power have I to hurt or help?' and again—of the suffering German people—'They brought it on themselves.' Yet these thoughts, interacting, again condemn us, since the majority of these German people had, individually, as little power as I to control their rulers; and still we dare to account them responsible. By some of the best among them that responsibility is accepted: 'True', say the authors of the Stuttgart Declaration, 'we have struggled for many years in the name of Jesus Christ against the spirit which has found its terrible

[1] Quoted in *Gladstone and the Irish Nation* by J. L. Hammond (Longmans, 1938), p. 104.
[2] Written in 1946.

expression in the National Socialist régime of violence, but we accuse ourselves for not having been more courageous'; and they speak of acknowledging with their people 'a solidarity of guilt'.[1] Equally we all, of the victor nations, are challenged to know ourselves participant in any collective action whose vindictive callousness may ensure—as did that defeated violence—present and future suffering.

It is a new and baffling dimension of morality that opens before us through this quickened sense of responsibility on the part of the individual for actions of a whole of which he is an insignificant member. Apart from the extreme difficulty such an individual has in obtaining knowledge of the facts dealt with, he lacks direction by any generally accepted moral outlook such as may obtain in regard to individual relationships. In his searching study of the life of the Capuchin Friar, *Grey Eminence*, Huxley has commented on the lack of guidance which Father Joseph's religious upbringing afforded in regard to the most difficult of moral problems—those concerned with acts performed on behalf of some social organization, such as a nation, a church, a political party. 'Too many Christian moralists', Huxley observes, have ignored these problems, as did those religious teachers to whom he attributes part responsibility for the evils of the Friar's political career.[2]

The negative pessimistic attitude which Huxley himself expresses towards all political activity appears related to his

[1]   The Stuttgart Declaration read by Bishop Wurm, at the Synod of the Evangelical Church of Germany, on 19 October 1945, was quoted in the Christian News-Letter of 20 February 1946.

The recognition of collective responsibility here considered must be seen as compatible with what has been described as 'the endless gradations of guilt and innocency which lie between the overt evil-doers and those who overtly resisted them' in a nation judged guilty such as Nazi Germany. The 'solidarity of guilt' which the Declaration recognizes belongs to the religious attitude achieved through prayer and contemplation; it is on a different plane from necessary practical judgements concerning guilt and innocence. The point urged above is that religious insight concerning collective responsibility has received from recent events a new range and intensity.

[2] *Grey Eminence*, p. 68.

concept of the experience of God—of Ultimate Reality—
as requiring 'abstraction from all creatures'. 'Mystical
philosophy', he states, 'can be summed up in a single
phrase "The more of the creature, the less of God".' This
principle he regards as ensuring condemnation of all activity
on a large scale, 'involving the collaboration of great
numbers of individuals in every stage of unenlightenment'.
Such activities 'are almost wholly creaturely; therefore they
almost wholly exclude God'.[1] That political action is always
foredoomed to a partial if not complete self-stultification
will, Huxley thinks, be realized empirically if we consider
the many instances of 'reforms upon which well-intentioned
people have placed the most enormous hopes'—such reforms
as universal education and public ownership of the means of
production. The first, attempted in Britain, the second in
Russia, have each failed lamentably to produce the results
expected.

In relation to these most difficult problems of large-scale
collective action there seems distinctive relevance in such a
concept as Whitehead's of the Divine persuasion. Huxley is
surely right in his contention[2] that the theory of Providence,
if so held as to suggest that history with its grievous record
of conflict and cruelty is 'an expression of the Divine will',
can bring only bewilderment to conscience. Also it is true
that the large-scale action of statesmen requiring collaboration of individuals full of creaturely egoism must have
consequences disappointing to romantic hopes. Yet we may
perhaps moderate such hopes without falling into despair of
creaturely efforts when we reflect on the patience of God in
action upon measureless recalcitrance, and consider the
ages past reckoning needed to fashion a creature that could
so much as conceive the relation, *I-Thou*. Now, when at
last there has emerged from the animal order, with its jungle
law of force and cunning, a creature conceiving the law of

[1] *ibid.* pp. 240, 242.　　　[2] *op. cit.* p. 241.

fellowship, capable at its best of serving as God's conscious agent in the world, we cannot wonder that the world still yields slowly to this creaturely transmission of the divine purpose.

Dismissing the idea of Providence which makes God responsible for the course of history, we may still value thought of the foreknowledge—foreseeing—implied in the divine omniscience. If even to God the future as influenced by creaturely freewill remains uncertain, yet our own scanty knowledge of the world's course permits some foreseeing of its outcome. Much more must that intimate awareness of all processes, conscious and inanimate, which we attribute to God include far-reaching foresight of results.

It is perhaps, above all, upon the scope of divine knowledge and intention that the stress must fall of religious thought concerned with these world problems. Corresponding to the growth of knowledge of physical and mental process, corresponding also to our quickened sense of responsibility in world relationship, should be a keener, more continuous awareness of the divine intention, as harmonious fulfilment of potentialities discernible within an actual world full of conflict and frustration.

Accepting this idea of the divine intention, our need is to find images that in some measure exemplify it even within our disordered contemporary world. To the present writer one such image appears in the accounts given by David Lilienthal and others of the American T.V.A. (Tennessee Valley Authority) experiment. That 'men may learn to work in harmony with the forces of nature', using not 'despoiling what God has given' is part of the faith which, in the preface to his book, Lilienthal declares he has seen 'take on substance' in the developing life of the Valley through the progress of the experiment.[1] In contrast with

[1] *T.V.A.: Democracy on the March* by David E. Lilienthal. (Penguin Book, 1944), p. 11.

the terrible picture presented in some recent records[1] of reckless exploitation and destruction of natural resources we have, in the accounts of T.V.A., assurance that men armed with all new resources of power can live not as bandits on the earth but respecting the nature and needs of the soil and its growths. In his first outline of the story he has to tell, Lilienthal speaks of 'waters once wasted and destructive' now controlled to human purposes, 'of fields grown old and barren . . . now vigorous with new fertility . . . of forests that were hacked and despoiled now protected and refreshed with strong young trees'. (p. 13.)

Throughout the record, for all its practical tone, there is a spirit that may remind the reader of Buber's suggestion, conveyed in his poetic and philosophic terms, that the *I-Thou* relation is in some manner possible between man and such natural objects as a tree, a river. Buber's insistence, in his example, is upon encounter between the whole human personality and the whole being of the tree—its form, structure, and environmental relations—felt as a unity. Similarly throughout Lilienthal's book emphasis is on the unity of a whole region. Concern is with the river valley in every aspect of its being—its relation with the physical forces of rain, wind, sun, with the needs and forces of plant and animal life; above all, with the powers of its human inhabitants as complete persons, co-operatively contriving, ordering, enjoying.

Great as is the value of an example of community life organized in harmony with the order of nature, applying new knowledge to the use and conservation of natural resources, yet greater is our need for instances showing the conflicts that embitter human relations in some measure

[1] I refer to such records of soil erosion as appear in *The Rape of the Earth*, by Jackson Whyte; also to the facts dramatically presented in Steinbeck's novel, *Grapes of Wrath*—facts confirmed in such a book as *Ill Fares the Land*, by C. MacWilliams, dealing with the disastrous effects on workingmen's lives of exploitation of natural resources by owners caring only for quick financial returns.

overcome. An essential part of the faith that 'took on substance' through the history of the Tennessee Valley was in the method of democracy—the method Lilienthal calls 'grass roots administration'—as able to secure, for purposes of general welfare, agreement and active participation of those affected, overcoming the clash of private interests.

By 'democracy at the grass roots' is meant a method of decentralization that shall liberate and use the distinctive energies of individuals. 'The task', Lilienthal writes, 'of harmonizing and from time to time adjusting the intricate detailed maze of pieces that make up the unified development of resources in a world of technology, is something that simply cannot be done effectively from some remote government or business headquarters.' (p. 73.) Technical knowledge had to be taken to thousands of actual farms, applied voluntarily by individual farmers, so that they and their neighbours could see for themselves the bearing of the new knowledge on their individual problems.[1]

Not to farmers only but to industrial workers and the business men of the region these democratic methods are applied and found effective in achieving agreement. When clashes of interest, Lilienthal writes, can be 'examined on the spot, at the time they occur', consultation may discover practicable solutions before the conflict has become an issue 'encrusted in prejudice . . . the subject of slogans and crusades'. (p. 107.) Experts who live with the people's problems win from them, it is found, confidence that is a protection against partisan attacks (p. 110).

Inevitably not all conflicts between interests can be happily adjusted. Although the Authority's concern for the

---

[1] See the interesting description, given by Lilienthal (*op. cit.* Ch. IX) and by Julian Huxley (*T.V.A.: Adventure in Planning*, Architectural Press, 1943, pp. 34-49) of 'demonstration farms' and 'demonstration areas', showing how methods of persuasion, the provision of opportunity through advice and help, overcame suspicion, winning the confidence first of an enterprising few, then of many more through observation of the results achieved.

needs and feelings of individuals caused them to make expert help available for everyone whose way of life was disturbed by the new constructions,[1] and careful records were kept of 'family adjustments', only a certain percentage—seventy per cent., Lilienthal estimates—of the families obliged to move 'expressed themselves as better or equally well satisfied in their new locations' (p. 62). The question arising in a reader's mind as to the families unsatisfied, the thirty per cent., recalls one to the inevitable limitation of the harmony that can be achieved in human affairs. Yet even with such limitations allowed for—the existence of residual conflicts to which a report such as Lilienthal's gives little prominence— the story of T.V.A. holds enough of achievement, material and spiritual, to be a source of inspiration in our troubled time.

It is on record[2] that in 1942 a gunner on leave in Palestine, coming from grim action in Libya, wrote of the Jewish settlement in which he had spent seven days: 'They have set a great example of what God made the world for.' Similarly, one oppressed by daily arriving news of conflict and devastation, turning to a record such as Lilienthal's, of so much achieved reconciliation of men with each other and with the forces of nature, may find in it a moving example of the Divine intention—an image through which he may encounter God present even within the tangled mesh of human affairs.

How far is it possible that the methods employed in

[1] An illustration of the extent of the disturbance of community life caused by the constructions necessary for flood control, and the success of the methods of consultation employed, is the account Lilienthal gives of what happened at the small town of Guntersville. Here the building of one of the main river dams necessitated the flooding of a number of streets in the town's business section. The townsfolk naturally felt strong objection; but consultation between city officials and the Authority's planning technicians resulted in an agreed plan whereby profitable use was made of the invading water, and the town became both a thriving port and an attractive recreation centre. A 'community sense of direction', Lilienthal adds, 'has resulted that continues to bear fruit' (p. 63).

[2] In *Palestine Controversy, a Symposium* (Fabian Publications, 1945), p. 26.

reconciliation of conflicting interests in the Tennessee Valley can be extended to allay more desperate conflicts in other areas of the world? References to T.V.A. methods—either hopeful or doubtful almost to despair—may be met with in many discussions of world problems. The idea 'of the planned development of natural regions such as river valleys has already found its way', says Julian Huxley, 'into the world's general thinking'.[1] So also has the idea of the Corporation invested with wide powers for fulfilment of a particular function that transcends the power of existing political agencies—states or nations.

The thinker without the wide and technical knowledge necessary to estimate projects inspired by these ideas may yet learn of them with hope that the influence on men's attitudes of planning together to meet our time's desperate needs may prove—as Lilienthal says it did in his experience —'the most important result of all', perhaps even, as another great public servant has suggested, a beginning of world co-operation and peace.[2]

VIII

These are precarious hopes, and faith is sustained with difficulty in a Divine influence operative through collective action. We may turn with relief to a question more familiar in religious thought: that concerning encounter with God in the individual life. We have spoken already of such encounter within the life of service between man and man. But according to traditional religious faith there is another form of encounter with God, by the spirit in its aloneness,

[1] *T.V.A.: Adventure in Planning*, p. 135.
[2] In the radio talk by Sir John Boyd Orr presenting his 'Food Plan' (recorded in *The Listener*, 26 September 1946), this plan of the World Food Board is described as doing something 'even more important' than lifting men out of their material poverty. It 'would help to bring about world unity'. By working together on this 'plan which brings no fear', the nations may achieve a 'co-operation which would be the beginning of one world government' and the 'only sure foundation for world peace'.

through meditation and through prayer. Is prayer possible
to such a faith as that indicated above—a faith lacking the
confidence of that simple child-to-father relation by which
prayer has been often sustained?

To focus thought here I take an instance of prayer quoted
by a writer who hardly ventures to conceive in personal
terms encounter with the Divine. In *One Kind of Religion*, by
Dr. Helen Wodehouse, there is a description and 'analysis
of a particular worked out prayer',[1] seeming to centre in the
words, *Thy Will be done*. These words, to all familiar with
the great Christian archetype, echo from the Lord's Prayer,
and, with yet deeper tragic meaning, from the agony of
Gethsemane: *Thy Will, not mine*. The concern of the individual whose story of his prayer Dr. Wodehouse quotes was
with a typically present-day commonplace situation—choice
by a committee among candidates for a vacant post—but
the need prompting the prayer was still, as in that supreme
example, for surrender to a higher Will of the separate
bodily will, instinct-dominated.

The mood from which his prayer sprang, this writer tells
us, was becoming 'hot and excited and bitter', as failure was
foreseen to persuade colleagues to choose the man who, in
the writer's judgement, was best fitted for the post. The
intention of the prayer, at this moment of 'cramped' personal desire, was to widen vision, to recall the situation's
demand for respect by each for the judgement of others,
and the need for fellowship and helpfulness, even if mistaken
choices are made and cherished hopes frustrated.

The prayer seemed 'an intent conversation', carried on
in 'voices speaking . . . to me or through me'; 'the experience
was not that of looking at myself and doing things to
myself', but of looking out from the situation in 'a definite
direction. The happenings that followed might well be
described as "The Lord said".' Yet his thought, the writer

[1] *One Kind of Religion* (Cambridge University Press, 1944), pp. 68 and 70.

tells us, of the Lord who spoke, was not of a person, but rather of 'Truth and Good, and the craving after truth and good, somehow speaking for themselves'.

I would ask any reader whose thought-image of God is of a person, a mind like that of a human helper—teacher, father—responding to his own, does this formulation under the terms, Truth, Good, of the Power that responds to prayer, take from prayer its meaning and reality?

In a review of Dr. Wodehouse's book, written, it would seem in the heat of feeling, by Cuthbert Lattey, S.J.,[1] the terms Dr. Wodehouse uses—the same employed in the prayer she quotes—are described as 'no more than sounding brass and tinkling cymbal to heart and mind'; she writes, it is said, 'of a religion that is no religion, prayer that is no prayer'.

Knowing the almost inevitable blindness of one mind, passionate within its own conditioned form of faith, to another conditioned to a different form, one can well understand this vehement rejection. Yet by another adherent of the Catholic faith, a further-reaching magnanimity is found possible towards those differing from him in the thought-images of their approach to God. 'To every soul', writes Jacques Maritain, Divine grace offers in some form 'that Reality of absolute goodness which merits all our love and is able to save our life . . . and if this grace is not rejected . . . the soul in question, in its choice of that reality, believes obscurely in the true God and really chooses Him, even where it conceptualizes this faith in the true God under formulas that deny Him.'[2]

Speaking from within an outlook, that, unlike Maritain's, recognizes no absolute revelation of God and truth, the present writer accepts his faith that to every human spirit a choice between good and evil is offered under forms

---

[1] In the *Hibbert Journal*, April 1945.
[2] *True Humanism* (translated by M. R. Adamson. Centenary Press, 1938), pp. 56-7.

‿onditioned by his individual life-history and his heredity physical and social. The reality of prayer, and of religion, is in the choosing, the reaching out towards a Reality indicated however obscurely under the images of good inherited by that spirit.[1]

To the individual whose story of his prayer was quoted the image his problem defined was of good expressed in relations of helpfulness, harmonized wills, beyond the scope of his present feeling. The words used at the time were, he says, like 'handholds in climbing'. Those central words, *Thy will be done*, were, one divines, handholds more secure for their long history of use in the spiritual ascent of man. Every thinking man, T. S. Eliot has asserted, 'must have his own scepticism', and this scepticism though it may end in denial, may also lead to faith, and be 'somehow integrated into the faith that transcends it'.[2] The scepticism which for many minds to-day turns to myth[3] or image what was once to many the central fact of history, can, when such scepticism is sincere and inevitable, be integrated into faith. Then, together with the great archetype of the Divine Will and vision, the image of the life surrendered to that Will, dying and rising again from death, remains an inspiration and support, a handhold in prayer and the adventuring of the human spirit.

The effect of prayer on the individual who prays can be, in principle, grasped by our reason. If the Divine *Thou* my

[1] Though the image, or concept, of Good as 'a concrete Universal' offered in *One Kind of Religion* appears that of a deeply sincere religious thinker, yet it seems to me that the spirit that cannot believe its prayer to address a *Thou* of conscious all-embracing wisdom has lost from the archetype of God that character which gives fullness of meaning not only to prayer, but to all striving after a truth beyond that required by merely practical needs.

[2] *Essays Ancient and Modern* (Faber, 1936), p. 151.

[3] I use the term 'myth' in the sense given to the word by Berdyaev and by Reinhold Niebuhr: religious myth is a concrete expression 'of the relation between the finite and the eternal which cannot be completely rationalized'; 'since myth cannot speak of the trans-historical without using symbols and events in history as its forms of expression, it invariably falsifies the facts of history, as seen by science, to state its truth.' (*An Interpretation of Christian Ethics*. S.C.M. Press, 1936, pp. 23, 24.)

prayer addresses is ever more ready to give aid towards good than I am to receive, limited in giving only by limitations of my mind and brain, then my prayer's function is to widen channels of reception. My spirit turning to God, striving with all resources of memory and imagination to survey its own action and situation as with the divine vision, may open, if ever so little, those brain paths that condition and limit reception of Grace. My faith that this is possible, that such a *Thou* does meet my spirit and co-operate with my prayer, does not warrant me in believing that prayer can influence processes where the mysterious relation of spirit to body does not hold. That my prayer could have any effect, for instance, on weather conditions I cannot believe. There may, indeed, be times when a natural impulse moves me to what I cannot but think of as pseudo-prayer: *O God avert this happening I so much dread. Let that happen which I desire.* Such a cry becomes true prayer only if the spirit's reaction follows: *If this that outrages my body's will must be, give me wisdom and strength to meet it.*

Can that faith whose integrated scepticism forbids prayer for external happenings, offer with sincerity prayer for beings other than the one who prays? Can I, praying for another spirit's strengthening and enlightenment, believe my prayer can widen channels of reception in another nature?

Let us again focus thought by an instance of prayer in present-day conditions—an instance taken this time from poetic drama.

In the play by Auden and Isherwood, *The Ascent of F*.6, there is a prayer which seems to stand at the centre of the play's problem—that of an individual inwardly revolting against the community he serves, and against the motives of his own acceptance of that service. This man, Ransom, has undertaken to lead a climbing expedition which those in authority believe will have a favourable effect upon their country's fortunes. All through the play, even to his death in the hour of his achieved ascent, Ransom's mind is bitter with conflict—with his contempt for those who sent him, contempt also for his own weakness that yielded, and dread of the half-recognized craving in himself for the rôle of popular hero. Only in the moment of prayer is the bitterness lightened, with an effect in the play as of clouds scattered, unveiling a serene heaven, an influence from another sphere. Ransom prays:

> O you, who are the history and the creator
> Of all those forms in which we are condemned to suffer;
> To whom the intelligent and the necessary is also the just;
> Show me my path, show all of us, that each upon
> This mortal star may feel himself the danger
> That under his hand is softly palpitating.
> Quicten that hand, interpret fully the commands
> Of the four centres and the four conflicting winds.
> Those torn between the charities, O reconcile.
> And to the human vision lead of one great meaning,
> Linking the living and the dead, within the shadow
> Of which uplifting, loving and constraining power
> All other reasons do rejoice and operate.

In this prayer, in the first group of lines and the last, an attempt is made to express that Power never to be expressed adequately—the *Thou* of the supreme encounter. The words, *you, who are the history and the creator Of all those forms in which we are condemned to suffer*, to me seem apt to express the thought philosophers have shaped of the Power through whom successive types of order appear within the aboriginal flux, God himself not maker only, but immanent in these forms—their history—suffering with his creatures, yet transcendent, a present knowledge of all that has been and can be. Such dwelling on one's thought of the Divine may, as in this prayer, quicken faith for that leap of the will beyond oneself to meet the Power that gives strength and vision. Here in the moment of will, the spirit, conscious of unity with others, craves enlightenment also for them: *show all of us*. Conscious, in the vivid image here offered, of the bodily self as danger—*under his hand palpitating*, like a lurking animal, its form unseen, only its secret urgency experienced—the spirit would lift all life with its own towards God who can subdue and harmonize conflicting winds and centres of desire.

Behind the prayer for 'all souls', says Cowper Powys, 'is an impulse to recognize and strengthen the tragic bond that unites the separate living consciousnesses of this whole present dimension'.[1] It is the sense of this tragic bond that perhaps justifies to our reason the prayer for other beings. Beneath the separateness of individuals runs the deep current, recognized in prayer, of our spirits' common need for liberation, inner harmony, enlightenment.[2]

IX

The faith that makes possible conscious meeting with God in this life generates a hope for perfected meeting on the other side of death. This hope, like the faith in meeting under present life-conditions, must assume individual form. It is perhaps in old age, as the certainty of death draws nearer, that the question of the spirit's destiny grows more urgent. One asks: What do I believe concerning this change that approaches? What ground have I for so believing?

Of her hero's belief in 'the immortality of the spirit' a contemporary novelist has written: 'He found that he was sure of it as he was of breath. The thought didn't bring him any pleasure. It was, like the war, a hard necessity which

---

[1] *The Art of Growing Old* (Cape, 1944), p. 128.
[2] A phrase used by Stephen Spender seems to me significant where he speaks of having been, during the time of separation through the war, 'united to friends in France and to friends in Europe by what amounted to bonds of prayer' (*European Witness*. Hamish Hamilton, 1946, p. 102). This, I take it, is a reference to the deep continuous desire and intention related to a common ideal, by which friends may be united in a manner similar to that 'tragic bond' uniting all souls, though more closely with each other than with those not sharing such conscious relationship.

you might, or might not, wish to accept, but which had to be endured. . . . Vaguely he tried to test his own belief to find out how he had arrived at it. But it seemed as impossible as to measure love or to reason against hate.'[1]

The immortality here spoken of remains undefined. From the context it appears that this strong belief, discovered almost with surprise, was linked with no recollected teaching from childhood. If I question my own belief, I seem to find, similarly, an assurance quite alien from early picturing of heaven and hell, a ground-belief—more like a necessity than a hope—arising from the distinction I find inevitable, between the *I*, the knower, correlative of all the world as known, and the particular body and brain with its needs and habits, so unaccountably found to be the vital station of this knower, its medium of interaction with the world and other selves.

Philosophic justification can be attempted for this distinction, but I speak here only on the level of spontaneous intuitive thought.

Looking backward through the ages before personal memories begin, A. E. Housman comforts his spirit with the thought of long oblivion:

> Men loved unkindness then, but lightless in the quarry
> I slept and saw not; tears fell down, I did not mourn;

Yet are we so certain? Truly this body, my present station, had not from the vast quarry of material existence gathered into life; it is another question whether the spirit, that which knows and wonders in me now, slept and saw not. Millions have believed otherwise.

'It has always been a puzzle to me', writes an Indian philosopher,[2] 'why European thinkers—apart from Theosophists—have not been attracted to the Karma theory' as

[1] *The Sycamore Tree*, by E. Cambridge, 1934.
[2] A. R. Wadia in *Contemporary Indian Philosophy*, edited Muirhead, 1936.

E

explaining our individual position in the world. In *The Summing Up*, the English novelist, Somerset Maugham, has confessed how strongly this doctrine of Karma has attracted him, as the 'one explanation [of life's meaning and sufferings] which appealed equally to my sensibility and to my imagination'. If the spirit passes from life to life and the apparently arbitrary dealing out to the individual, through his inherited resources and station at birth, of the chances of wisdom and happiness were due in part to that spirit's choices in past lives; if, also, the efforts and endurances of the present life can influence the opportunities of a life in the future, our sense of justice would be less outraged. Existence would be cleared, Maugham thinks, 'of the meaninglessness of pain which is pessimism's unanswered argument'. Yet he adds: 'I can only regret that I find the doctrine impossible to believe.'

To the present writer it seems strange—with that strangeness inevitable in another's differing intimate outlook—that the belief so grasped and commended should appear impossible to accept. For me the waking after death to another life on earth seems not a certainty indeed, yet, almost probably, a necessity to be endured. To one whose besetting weakness has been fear of life's vicissitudes, who has felt horror at others' suffering, belief that one must plunge again amid the chances of mortal life is far from offering any cheer or allurement. Yet concerning it the thought springs ever to mind: once having wakened so unaccountably to this present life, how should I not expect—so far as one can 'expect' anything—again to waken with no more memory of the past, or understanding how or why?

This background of belief is no matter of faith or hope; but against it there rises the hope of which I have spoken as generated by religious faith. If, between the wakenings, there might be meeting—more adequate than is possible in earthly life—with God, the source of meaning, one might

gain the courage that human destiny demands. The best
thing in this life has been not its pleasures and bodily
comforts but the dim sense of meaning that through it all
has been never completely, though sometimes nearly, lost.
If, after death, one could look back on life, seeing its relations with other lives, its efforts and failures, mistakes and
groping, all completed within the divine intention, every
glimpse of meaning fully illumined, the life thus known
would be worth more than its cost in suffering; and lives to
be endured in the future might be through that vision
lighted more fully than this has been, strengthened, one
would dare to hope, by a more constant sense of relation to
the Divine.

Of this longed for vision of life's truth we have faint
intimations in present experience; in moments of contact
with minds wiser than our own, or in those times when by
unaccountable illumination present and past perplexities
stand clear to us. Also, of this vision we inherit images from
poets, saints, philosophers. Plato has told of the place above
the heavens where the Divine Part of the soul is quickened
and fed with knowledge in its essential being, and how when
the soul from that heavenly place falls to earth, some love
and longing stays with it for truth and beauty it once knew.
Dante, through successive stages of his *Paradiso*, has built up
an image of radiance significant of every value of human love
and insight, so that, at his poem's climax, that single point of
intensest light 'where every *where* and every *when* is focused'
may be felt by every responsive reader as symbol of the Divine
meaning by which his own life is haunted. Augustine has
left record of the moment of transcendent awareness that
for him gave reality to his thought of Eternal life.

There is one image nearer to our time than these, in which
I find peculiar value through its alliance of verbal imagery
with music, and because it offers imaginative representation
of a whole experienced passage through pains of death and

wonder of changed state to the divine vision and judgement, and from this to accepted exile for growth and expiation through renewed suffering. I refer to Newman's poem, *The Dream of Gerontius*, especially to the poem as rendered in abbreviated form with Elgar's music—its doctrinal element thus subordinated, its emotional, imaginative values heightened. In this form the definite imagery of the Catholic faith presents no obstacle to one outside that Church. I, equally with the Catholic believer, may know in death an 'innermost abandonment', an 'emptying out of each constituent, And natural force by which I come to be'; and from that mortal weakness may cry to the Eternal Strength:

> Sanctus fortis, Sanctus Deus
> De profundis oro te.

For me the supreme moment of *Gerontius* as interpreted by Elgar's music is that of the coming of the soul before its judge. The words chosen—

> O happy suffering soul! for it is safe
> Consumed, yet quickened, by the glance of God—

serve as expression of the thought of the whole individual life summed up, realized with all its possibilities in the Divine intention, and with the spirit's consuming anguish for its falling short of these. The soul's cry,

> Take me away, and in the lowest deep
> There let me be,

tells of the eager acceptance of purgation in 'penal waters'; but for those of us who find no need to postulate other place of penal suffering than this troubled earth, that cry expresses well our willingness to suffer again, on earth or elsewhere, whatever is required for atonement or fulfilment, if only sense of Divine meaning be not lost to us.

In the *Life of Gervase Elwes* (by W. and R. Elwes. Grayson, 1935) a letter is quoted written to him by one who declares himself 'not a Catholic', saying that up till the time of hearing this singer's sincere rendering of *Gerontius*, 'the fear of death had been a source of great trouble and distress to me: neither prayer nor reason helped me in the least, and the subject was one I could not face. The night I heard *The Dream of Gerontius*, a new vision came to me and the whole point of view was changed; it was as though a great burden of darkness and horror fell away and light and peace took their place'. The writer observes that this change, which at the time of writing had persisted for more than a year with only 'added assurance', was inexplicable to him. To me it seems an illustration of the power of a vivid image expressing something that the individual spirit has been ready to feel and believe, but which has lacked embodiment.

It is right, Plato asserts in the *Phaedo*, in regard to an image of the future life of which we know nothing with certainty, to use a myth, a likely tale, as a 'charm', a 'lure' to draw out the potentialities of the soul.

The likelihood of the tale told by the mythical image, when to any individual it serves as charm and lure, must depend on some relation between it and the individual history and resources. For other minds other images than those I have referred to may better embody the great archetype of the heavenly place and state. But for all, I think, the need remains, whether keenly or barely recognized, for some imagery giving shape to the wonder at what may be beyond the confines of earthly life.

x

In closing this essay and again putting to myself the question why I should ask for my individual thought the attention of other minds, I turn to that hope for the world, for mankind on this planet, that—like hope for the spirit leaving this world—springs from faith in God. If in this life on earth there is Divine purpose, it seems unlikely that progress in mastery of material things will for ever so far outrun spiritual understanding and the discipline of the will. Some newly effective religious synthesis and vision may be taking shape amid the present confusion, decay of forms that once satisfied men's minds and dismay at the pass to which material achievement has brought us. If it is possible that one's individual thought should make any contribution to that sorely needed rebirth of spiritual tradition, one must try, even at an unlikely venture, to make that contribution.

Unlikeliness in my own venture might be due to my comparative isolation from the stresses of the present time. Yet I do not really think our individual minds are so separate as that fear would imply. Ideas shaped by the experience of many minds, whether consciously communicated or not, help to determine the issues present to an individual consciousness, so that one finds the discoveries of one's individual thought confirmed in the testimony of those who have endured, at shorter range, the shock of world events. So it is, I think, with the main thesis of this essay: that the Divine source of our being is encountered by us through no single unique revelation, but individually by different modes of approach; and therefore the great need of our time, as concerns religion, is for sincerity in our own faith, and, for the differing forms of others' faith, imaginative respect.

'The one value that remains to us in the collapse of values is sincerity.' I take this assertion from the discourse of one who experienced the full impact, both of Nazi aberration and of war with its effects. Speaking at the inauguration of medical courses at Heidelburg University, August 1945, Professor Jaspers referred to the deep confusion left in men's minds by all the devilry practised and endured in recent years, and to the lack of any common outlook, or 'ground on which we can stand in our conversation with one another'. Yet the very attempt at a rebuilding of university life implies, he recalled, a certain active faith in the rights of man, present in both victors and vanquished. It is for the members of the university to recreate its life by recovering the spirit of science and humanity—the scientific spirit as a continual criticizing and testing of all supposed knowledge, the spirit of humanity as respect for the whole man in his relation to God, making possible a fellowship that intellectual conflict does not destroy.[1]

It is the twofold requirement thus indicated as essential to spiritual renewal that I have tried to illustrate from the resources of my own life and study; speaking, first, of those forms of imagery of the Divine—ancient and well-nigh universal—which we may term archetypal; then of the possibility of discriminating by the use of reason between more and less valid forms of such imagery—a use of reason essential for those who cannot accept any revelation as uniquely authoritative, given once for all.

I think one main motive of this essay is the desire to communicate some sense of the value which those not accepting a once-for-all revelation may still experience both in the great archetypes, and in those historic instances which distinctively enshrine them. Discrimination between forms traditionally presented of the ideas of God and Christ is not an impertinence if its intention is to realize those ideas in their true value for oneself, in one's own station and moment of history. Emphasis is not on negation, but on the need that effective belief be liberated from any stifling weight of untested half-belief. It seems likely that some who might have found value in the great archetypes of religion have rejected them for lack of any critical sincere examination of the forms in which they have been presented. Such minds

[1] Professor Jaspers' address is published as Supplement to *The Christian News-Letter*, 14 November 1945.

have been content perhaps with obvious criticisms of religious images, not testing them for an underlying truth. So testing, they might have found expression given to the meaning of that 'silent partner' whose influence is felt in our secret dialogue with ourselves.

Arthur Koestler, in his powerful novel, *Darkness at Noon*, has given to the phrase, 'silent partner' in inner dialogue, a significance relevant to our present question of the value of religious archetypes—their value, especially, to those unsatisfied by the dogmas of any church. Koestler has depicted the struggle in the mind of Rubashov, an adherent of the Russian Communist party, as he comes to realize values that his communist creed ignores. In the struggle of Rubashov's whole nature, feeling and intellect alike, towards understanding of life, the 'silent partner' remains inarticulate, yet thrusts into the focus of thought particular memories, images that point him to unrealized truths. It is, I think, in the same way that images present in religious and poetic tradition—such images as those of a divine birth, death and resurrection—point towards truth which our incarnate spirits need, but which beliefs dictated by scientific aims and short-range practical necessities easily ignore.

At an earlier point in this essay I illustrated from Saint Exupéry's *Flight to Arras* the union in a present-day experience of imagery and feeling rooted far back in racial history with philosophic thought keenly contemporary and reaching out into the future. This example suggested the question: could such complete action of the powers of personality be any guarantee that the experience was indeed an encounter with the Divine? Now as an outcome of the whole argument of this essay, I would venture to answer the question. If we dare to believe that within this mortal life our spirits encounter the Divine, it must be, I think, most truly at those times when our whole nature is active, feeling, intellect, will; or if at the moment of meeting—as many mystics have declared—all activity seems stilled, yet into that stillness has passed the resultant of action, the striving of the whole personality, both of the individual and of innumerable lives whose groping insight has shaped the images that direct our search for God.

I end this essay as I began, with recurrence to remembered youth. One night, when my mind had been occupied with this essay's theme, I dreamed of rising from bed and descending the stairs in my childhood home, going softly, with precaution not to disturb their sleep, past my parents' bed-chamber, down to the familiar living-room; meeting there the girl I once was—the same that, sitting with mother in the family pew, wondered at the hopeless unreality of the imagery through which was made to her the offer of salvation. I told this girl—or tried to tell her across the dividing years—that I had found what she despaired of finding. I woke then, and meditated, with thankfulness, that the dream had truth. I had found what for me was the meaning of that image of the hallowed figure that knocks on the door. Not alone the Jesus of the Gospel story, but others also, through records of past thought and deed or through speech and action in the present, convey to mortal ears—the doorway of the spirit—the challenge, the command, the consolation, of the Eternal.

Though the speech of my essay bears throughout the mark of my individual limitations—my bond with that bewildered child of the eighteen-eighties—yet its central thought, I believe, by recognizing, escapes subjectivity—the thought that each of us, through imagery and modes of experience that have truth for our individual being, may encounter the Divine.

II

THE IMAGE OF THE DIVINE BIRTH

THE SECOND COMING

Turning and turning in the widening gyre
The falcon cannot hear the falconer;
Things fall apart: the centre cannot hold;
Mere anarchy is loosed upon the world.
The blood-dimmed tide is loosed, and everywhere
The ceremony of innocence is drowned:
The best lack all conviction, while the worst
Are full of passionate intensity.

Surely some revelation is at hand:
Surely the Second Coming is at hand.
The Second Coming! Hardly are those words out
When a vast image out of Spiritus Mundi
Troubles my sight: somewhere in sands of the desert
A shape with lion body and the head of a man,
A gaze blank and pitiless as the sun
Is moving its slow thighs, while all about it
Reel shadows of the indignant desert birds.

The darkness drops again; but now I know
That twenty centuries of stony sleep
Were vexed to nightmare by a rocking cradle,
And what rough beast, its hour come round at last,
Slouches towards Bethlehem to be born.

I

THE poem by W. B. Yeats which I have set at the head of
my essay has been felt by many readers as significant in
relation to our time. For me it possesses that arresting
quality which, when we feel it in poetry, denotes the stirring
within us of deeply-felt elemental meanings such as we may
term archetypal.

The poem culminates in the last lines telling of the 'rough beast' that, at the destined hour, 'slouches towards Bethlehem to be born'. The name of Bethlehem, place of the birth from which we date our era, can of itself waken, though perhaps but faintly, thought of a holy incarnation— entry of a divine being into our human order. In these lines that idea is brought with something of felt shock into relation with a beast, a monster whose image is made at once vivid and unearthly through this slouching approach to the place in the world's memory consecrated to the admission of the transcendent.

Thus the theme of the poem is of a birth contrasted with that we think of as divine: a birth we may term *numinous*, using the word given currency by Rudolf Otto,[1] to characterize that which arouses awe, transcending, whether for good or ill, forces intelligible to our intellect. I have called my theme in this essay 'the image of the divine birth', for it is the image of the birth of Christ—to many of us made vivid from childhood through the Bible story, through poetry and pictures—that I take as the symbol on which our minds may rest, while we venture to consider also the more elusive idea, or archetype, suggested by Yeats' poem: the tendency to conceive, as breaking into our order for good or ill, a force from the unknown, transcendent, numinous.

In considering any poem that acts on us as a lure for thought and feeling we may distinguish the question, 'what does this poem communicate to me?' from the question, 'what can I discover concerning its meaning for the poet who wrote it?' Some hints of an answer to the second question can be found in other writings of Yeats, but let us, before noting these, consider in first outline what this poem —published in 1921—communicates to us to-day.

Anarchy 'loosed upon the world', 'the blood-dimmed tide', the best lacking conviction 'while the worst are full of

[1] In English translation, *The Idea of the Holy* (Oxford University Press, 1924).

passionate intensity': these phrases serve well to recall the horror come upon us through Fascist and Nazi violence, culminating in the war that so nearly destroyed our world. 'Surely the Second Coming is at hand!' In men's extremity, when the powers of evil seem let loose, the hope and longing wakens for deliverance; but as in our own lives such hope may encounter only new shapes of evil, so in the poem there follows a monstrous vision, a 'vast image' man-headed, lion-bodied, pitiless; then for the poet knowledge—for us, perhaps, a question—as to the relation of this birth to the centuries preceding it: is it to this nightmare of evil that the Christian hope has led, the hope symbolized by the cradle of Bethlehem, held in the minds of men whose earth-bound nature, unresponsive to the divine message, made of their linked lives a 'stony sleep'? As once for Christian faith Bethlehem became the point of intersection of two worlds, of time with timeless value, so has this present time become a new Bethlehem, a point of entry into human life of evil, again transcendent, beyond anything of which we had deemed our human nature capable?

Ideas and questions such as these the poem has suggested to me, and to others, reading and dwelling on it during and since the time of the last great war. Writing before that time, Yeats must have had in view earlier conditions of anarchy. Something of what was in his mind is indicated in the poem, *Nineteen Hundred and Nineteen*, in a verse referring to the Black and Tan terror:

> Now days are dragon-ridden, the nightmare
> Rides upon sleep: a drunken soldiery
> Can leave the mother murdered at her door
> To crawl in her own blood, and go scot-free;
> The night can sweat with terror, as before
> We pieced our thought into philosophy,
> And planned to bring the world under a rule,
> Who are but weasels fighting in a hole.

The horror thus described may well have opened a prophetic glimpse into future evils. In this poem, however, Yeats looks backward over history: *twenty centuries of stony sleep were vexed to nightmare by a rocking cradle.* The thought in these lines grows clearer when we relate them to other lines expressing his sense of the recalcitrance of the human heart haunted by an ideal that is its own opposite:

> Some violent bitter man, some powerful man,
> Called architect and artist in that they,
> Bitter and violent men, might rear in stone
> The sweetness that all longed for night and day,
> The gentleness none there had ever known.

This verse, applied directly to Irishmen of recent times, can serve also as commentary on Yeats' thought of the medieval cathedral builders, stony of heart and violent in action, challenged, 'vexed', by dreams of the birth of love. So again the lines:

> We had fed the heart on fantasies.
> The heart's grown brutal from the fare;
> More substance in our enmities
> Than in our love . . .[1]

could refer to that whole course of centuries that made of Christ's teaching an occasion of dispute and persecution, and led towards the catastrophes of our day.

Terrible as seems Yeats' vision of the man-headed monster arising at the Second Coming of the Transcendent into the world, the tone and strong movement of the poem suggest that whatever the monster of his vision symbolized was by him accepted without horror. By his prose writings this impression is confirmed. He had made for himself a pattern or framework of thought within which he could arrange historical happenings. Within this pattern of developing

[1] Both quotations from the poem, *Meditations in Time of Civil War.* 1923.

and interchanging tendencies he thought of the birth of
Christ as beginning an era when man's spirit looked 'beyond
itself towards a transcendent power', an era therefore
'dogmatic, levelling, unifying, feminine, humane'. In our
own time his pattern led him to expect the birth of an era
of opposite character, 'obeying inner power, hierarchical,
multiple, masculine, harsh, surgical.' 'Something of this',
he asserted, 'the new era must be'. Yet he adds 'always . . .
the unique intervenes, that which is called by everyman his
freedom',[1] and, saying this, he quotes from his own poem
the vision of the sphinx-like monster. Yeats must have
recognized—this passage suggests—a direct relation of his
poem to unique reality, independently of that dogmatic
pattern into which his prose writings attempt to fit history.
In any case we who inherit his poem may take it as standing
in its own right, a created thing addressing us through its
own potentialities.

'A great poem', Shelley cried in his language of exaltation,
'is a fountain for ever overflowing with waters of wisdom
and delight.' It is for every age and every individual to
take from it all 'that their peculiar relations enable them to
share'.[2] The same thought, more analytically developed,
presents the words and phrases of a poem as having each a
character and history such that within the poem their new
grouping creates new powers of evocation to be realized in
the minds of readers, each responding in some degree
differently, according to his individual contacts with the
operative word-meanings.

Here in this poem we are considering, are word-meanings
with tremendous history and evocative power, conjoined
within a distinctive and powerful rhythm. The intention of
this essay is to follow, so far as my own contacts allow, something of the history of these great words: the *Cradle* of
Bethlehem, the *Second Coming*; these in their relation to the

[1] *A Vision* (Macmillan, 1937), pp. 263, 302.   [2] *Defence of Poetry.*

rough beast, the sphinx-like monster, and to that unique present reality to which in the last resort our meanings must all refer.

II

If for our image of the Cradle of Bethlehem, the Divine Birth, we seek the source earliest in human history, we may find it in that ritual pattern which characterized the religions of ancient Egypt, Babylon, and Canaan. In this pattern of myth and ritual, the divine king, or god, about whom worship centres and the myth is told, dies and is reborn, his rebirth signifying and promoting renewed fertility of the earth, of his people, their crops and herds. Among earliest images of the 'rocking cradle'—rocking the hearts of worshippers with hope, fear, desire—might be that animal skin in which, we are told,[1] the representation of Osiris was wrapped, as a 'cradle' symbolizing the god's rebirth. Celebrating that imaged rebirth in the ancient ritual were dances and rejoicings in which the worshipper could feel his own vigour of life projected into the future, animating the newly risen god and the awakening earth-life of which the god was the symbol.

Of dances with this same intention we have record in the inscribed hymn found in Crete, of which Jane Harrison has written so fully.[2] Here the returning year-god is celebrated as the child Dionysus grown to young manhood, and the intention of the dance is made clear in the words of the song:

> leap for full jars, and leap for fleecy flocks and
> leap for fields of fruit and for hives to bring increase.[2]

Whether the returning god is thought of as young man or

---

[1] See the Essay by W. O. E. Oesterley in *The Labyrinth* (edited by S. H. Hooke. London, 1935), p. 145.

[2] In *Themis;* and in *Ancient Art and Ritual* (Home University Library, 1913), p. 116.

as infant, the motive of the ancient ritual was the same—in Jane Harrison's words, 'the intense world-wide desire that the life of nature which seemed dead should live again'.

This intense desire expressed by men in common, in accordance with a prescribed ritual, comes near to prayer. Yet it lacks an element which our present thought of prayer finds essential. Prayer as an act of the spirit implies need for something more than material welfare. In the later Orphic ritual, based upon the Dionysiac ritual of rebirth, the spiritual element has entered. The rebirth desired is not merely that of nature, of plant and animal life; it is also a rebirth of the worshipper himself. There has entered an awareness, however dim, of a self, an *I* that seeks relation with a *Thou*, and to achieve that relation, must be purified, reborn.

The 'cradle' that had its part in the ritual of the Orphic worship was now the *liknon* (Lat. *vannus*) the shovel-shaped object which could serve not only as child's cradle but also as basket for the fruit of the vinegrower, and winnowing-fan for the farmer's corn. So late as the time of Virgil we find mention of the 'mystic fan of Iacchus', mystic through the many meanings that had come to centre about it. Like the winnowing-fan of which the Hebrew prophets spoke—*Whose fan is in His hand and He will throughly purge His floor*—the winnowing basket in Orphic ritual was a symbol of purification of the worshipper, as corn is purified from the husk. It was the cradle also of the divine child, Dionysus, by whose death and rebirth in his mysteries the participant believed himself purified and saved. Also it held the fruit, gift of the wine-god who thereby gave, at the times permitted by religion, the ecstasy of intoxication.

Strange and barbarous the rites appear to us through which purification and union with the god was offered to the worshipper. Founded upon the wild Thracian cult, the

F

Orphic myth and ritual was full of reminiscence of intoxicated orgies, of frenzied dances and rendings of raw flesh.
Yet the entry of the new element, the realized need for
spiritual rebirth, marks an epoch in human history, and we
are concerned both to examine the earliest recorded expressions of this need, and to learn what we can concerning
the conditions of its emergence.

Doctrine which, it is said,[1] can be classed unhesitatingly
as Orphic is found both in the second Olympian Ode of
Pindar, and, more fully, in preserved fragments of the
Purifications by Empedocles. In both poems the soul is
conceived as having fallen, as penalty for sin, from the
region of light into the dark turbulence of mortal life,
passing through many stages of life animal and human, ever
an exile and a wanderer till the years of its penance shall
be over.

Of the actual 'purifications', or ceremonial remedies,
which, it seems, Empedocles' poem described, indications
in the fragments remaining are few and obscure. The part
of the poem of greatest interest to us is that illustrating the
new awareness of an indwelling spirit alien to the bodily
self and its earthly heritage. I quote from Cornford's translation: 'Of these [the fallen 'spirits that are heirs of everlasting life'] now am I also one, an exile from heaven and
a wanderer, having put my trust in raging strife.' 'I wept
and wailed when I saw the unfamiliar land . . . the joyless
land, where are murder and wrath and troops of other
spirits of evil, and parching plagues and putrefactions, and
floods roam in darkness through the meadow of Destruction.'
'From what honour, from what a height of bliss (was I cast
down) when I left (Olympus?) to wander here among
mortals.'[2]

---

[1] See F. M. Cornford's discussion of the two poems in *From Religion to
Philosophy* (Arnold, 1912), Ch. VI, § 120.
[2] *Fragments* 115, 118, 121, 119. Translated in *Greek Religious Thought*, by
F. M. Cornford (Dent, 1923).

Seeking the source of these ideas, scholars have found evidence of influence from the East. It seems certain that a consciousness which Dr. Rudolf Otto has described as that of 'supramundane reality' existed among those who prayed for 'pardon and guidance' in the prehistoric period of Aryan religion, whose traditions were taken up into the great syncretistic hymn book of the Veda.[1] The researches of Eisler have suggested that it was through Persia that such ideas from the Far East penetrated Greek thought. On Iranian soil the study of the stars, and speculation concerning their relation to human life, helped to give form to the doctrine of the heavenly descent of the soul and its possible return to the region whence it fell.[2]

When ideas from a foreign source take hold on the life of a community, there must be, as well as the mere contact, a readiness to receive, due to some kinship of need and feeling. The Dionysian worship in its earlier form may have served to create such preparedness for the new ideas grafted upon it in Orphic religion. There is a connexion, scholars have believed, between intoxication, through wine and through the wild dance-orgy, and belief in the divinity and immortality of the soul. When the individual who is becoming conscious in his ordinary life of separateness and limitation can look back on times of induced ecstasy, with experience of group unity and inflowing power, that contrast may help to give meaning to the doctrine of an immortal, indwelling spirit, exiled from God and able to return to him only through obedience to the precepts of religion.

In *Psyche*, the great work of Erwin Rohde,[3] evidence is put forward at length for this hypothesis of relation between states of ecstasy, variously induced, and belief in the divinity

---

[1] *The Kingdom of God and the Son of Man,* by Rudolf Otto (translated Filson & Woolf. Lutterworth Press, 1930), pp. 21, 23.
[2] Eisler's evidence is adduced in his book *Weltenmantel u. Himmelszelt,* Vol. ii, referred to by Cornford, *op. cit.* pp. 162, 178.
[3] First published 1893. (English translation by W. B. Hillis. Kegan Paul, 1925).

of the soul. To another line of thought and research[1] belongs insistence on the effects of group excitement in contrast with an increasing sense of individual separateness in ordinary life. Both hypotheses, connecting the dawn of spiritual awareness with orgiastic excitement, may, in some minds, cause troubled perplexity. Must we accept such originating conditions as these for beliefs we dare to hope are true? Are we to find, through all our study of a divine unbreaking, the presence of some bodily stress or infirmity conditioning insight, some mingling of folly with wisdom, evil with good?

So central to our theme this problem appears to me that I cannot at this point forbear to quote from a modern poet who expresses with eloquence such perplexed questioning. In the poem, *Dark Rapture*, by AE, the drunken ecstasy exciting wonder is that of a single wanderer, 'Babbling inarticulately along the road', 'Gazing with intoxicated imagination' on the dance of the stars:

> Ah! could that maddened will, those riotous senses break
> Into the astral ecstasy, for a moment feel
> The profundities? Did he offer his sin to the most High?
>
> .   .   .   .
>
> I heard him cry *God* in amazement, as if his eyes
> Saw through these reeling lights the one eternal Light.
> Was that madness of his accepted as sacrifice?

With these lines I should like to compare the strange play of Euripides, *The Bacchae*. Though no comment can be made with assurance by one unable to study the play adequately in the Greek, and aware of the differing interpretations of scholars, yet one may hazard a guess that the play expresses an attitude somewhat similar to that of AE's poem. Such spiritual ecstasy as the modern poet divined rising upon the squalor of an individual drunkard, Euripides seems to

[1] Developed by Durkheim in *Elementary Forms of the Religious Life* (English translation, 1915). Also G. Heard, *Social Substance of Religion*, 1931.

have recognized, similarly with wonder, amidst the cruelty and horror of the rites of Dionysus. The choruses convey this impression; also passages in the two speeches of the messenger:

> . . . O King
> Hadst thou been there, as I, and seen this thing
> With prayer and most high wonder hadst thou gone
> To adore this god whom now thou railst upon,

then, after the terribly inspired murder, the words that counsel to mortals humility before the inscrutable mysteries of the divine will.

III

In contrast with the earlier images, to us so obscure, of divine entry into human life, the image of Christ's birth at Bethlehem shines clear for us with associations from childhood. To the fashioning of that image medieval paintings have contributed as well as the Gospel stories, and other poetry—for me notably the *Nativity Ode* of Milton. The mother I picture in her mantle of heavenly blue, or of red, flame colour of adoring love; she bends above the manger-cradle where lies the sleeping babe with glory round his head. The oxen are standing by, while angels, white-robed and shining, keep watch above 'the courtly stable'. On either side of the picture are ranged the figures of the humble shepherds and of the Eastern kings bearing gifts to lay at the feet of the child.

The image in some such form as this, and the poetry and pictorial art that have fashioned it, are a treasured part of our religious heritage. Yet there is value also—value I think greater for our present need—in those images not visual but conceived with the aid of historical research and philosophic thought. Such thought-images will include all

we can learn concerning the contribution of different ages
towards faith in divine entry into human life. If we can no
longer hold as historic fact our image of the birth in the
stable of Bethlehem, with the worshipping shepherds summoned by angels, and the star-guided magi, we have
compensation in the historic and philosophic truths that
image can symbolize—the contribution that both homely
life and animal need, and the far-flung speculation of
Eastern sages, have made towards faith in immanent
divinity.

Let us then, for the building up, or analysis, of our
thought-image, consider first in what form Indian sages, in
the ancient poems that have come down to us, presented
the entry of the divine into human life.

In the *Ramayana*,[1] Vishnu, at the prayer of the other gods,
takes birth for the destruction of the demon, Ravana. The
god himself, in the form of a flaming tiger, announces his
coming to the king of whose four wives he is to be born in
the form of as many sons. As Rama, that son in whom the
divine essence appears chiefly incarnate, the god passes
through many adventures and at last slays the demon,
accomplishing the mission 'for which alone Vishnu had
taken human form'. Later in the story, in connexion with
its secondary theme of the theft by the demon, and recovery
by Rama, of his wife, Sita, the incarnate god suffers the
rebuke of other gods, descended to earth in their heavenly
form. They chide him for behaving to Sita 'after the
fashion of a mere man', when he is in reality a god, 'beyond
time', 'the slayer of all enemies . . . the refuge of all gods
and hermits', and may now, his mission accomplished,
ascend to heaven. Rama, however, remains on earth and

[1] The form of the story and the words quoted are taken from *Myths of the
Hindus and Buddhists* by Nivedita and Coomaraswamy (Harrap, 1913).
Of his 'condensed translation' of the *Ramayana*, A. K. Coomaraswamy
states that 'no episode or figure of speech has been added for which the
original does not afford authority'.

reigns ten thousand years. In his kingdom all things prosper; 'due rains fell and the winds were ever favourable, and there was no distress from sickness or from wild beasts, or from invasion, but all men were glad and merry'. At last the mighty Yoga, Time, comes to the palace. Once more Rama is recalled to his divinity: 'Do thou with thy brothers enter in again in whatsoever form thou wilt, who art the refuge of all creatures, and beyond the range of thought or speech, unknown to any, save thy Maya.' So Rama, with his brothers, as Vishnu, enters heaven.

Reading this tale of an incarnation, one loving the Christian story cannot but contrast its serious, devout simplicity with what seems the fairy-tale atmosphere of the Indian epic. Yet amidst the long poem's fantastic detail there are passages that even to a mind with alien heritage convey depth of meaning. When Rama is recalled to his divinity and answers at first: 'I know myself only as a man, Rama, the son of Datharatha . . . tell me who I am and whence I came', do not his words find an echo of inner questioning in the spirit of any man whether of east or west? They suggest the thought which, we are told,[1] it is the aim of the Indian sacred writing to convey: for every man the true end of life is that he should come to know the Divine Ground of his being, and identify himself therewith, subordinating 'the life of the outer man, the life of separative selfhood'.

Even the fantastic detail embroidering the story will have value to those for whom the myth has become part of their familiar medium of expression. When Mahatma Gandhi would awaken in his hearers the faith that can remove mountains, he cites the 'exhaustless strength' that Rama gave to Hanuman, the king of the monkey tribe, who in his devoted service to the hero-god, through the god's strength

[1] See Aldous Huxley's survey of the Perennial Philosophy, as taught in India. *Introduction* to the translation of the *Bhagavad-Gita* by Prabhavananda and Isherwood (Phoenix House, London, 1947).

'lifted the mountain and crossed the ocean'[1]. Gandhi spoke
of the 'indissoluble bond', like that uniting a man with his
wife, that he felt with Hinduism, and with the *Gita* and the
Ramayana, 'the only two books in Hinduism I may be said
really to know.'[1] To this feeling those of us can readily
respond who recognize such a bond with myths that have
become from childhood part of our own life.

The passage that in the *Gita* tells of divine incarnation
speaks perhaps more clearly to a Western reader than does
any passage in the *Ramayana*. The god, incarnate as Krishna,
reveals his divine nature to Arjuna whose charioteer he has
become:

> I am the birthless, the deathless,
> Lord of all that breathes.
> I seem to be born:
> It is only seeming,
> Only my Maya.
> I am still master
> Of my Prakriti
> The power that makes me.
>
> When goodness grows weak,
> When evil increases,
> I make myself a body.
>
> In every age I come back
> To deliver thc holy,
> To destroy the sin of the sinner,
> To establish righteousness.
>
> He who knows the nature
> Of my task and my holy birth
> Is not reborn
> When he leaves this body:
> He comes to me.

[1] *Mahatma Gandhi's Ideas*, by C. F. Andrews (Allen & Unwin, 1929),
pp. 40, 48.

Flying from fear,
From lust and anger,
He hides in me
His refuge, his safety:
Burnt clean in the blaze of my being,
In me many find home.[1]

Here one may recognize the same solemn, appealing note
that sounds in the words of Jesus: *Come unto me. I will give
you rest.* Yet the note alien to us is present also: the divine
birth is 'only seeming'. The invitation of Jesus is that of
one who, whatever the mystery of his being or the meaning
of his divine claim, yet lived at a place and time definite in
our human order, wearing a human form actual and com-
pulsive as our own.[2]

Such historic actuality is shared by the founder of the
Buddhist religion. The verdict of scholarship, that the
prince Siddhartha or Gautama, trod the earth of Northern
India in the fifth or sixth century B.C. appears as secure as
is the judgement concerning the time and place of the life
of Jesus. About the historic figure in the literature of
Buddhism, birth-legends have become established not unlike
those in the New Testament. The Buddha was miraculously
conceived; angels informed his human father of the coming
of the holy child and bade his mother rejoice when the
promise was fulfilled. On the day of his birth a Brahman
priest, 'the Buddhist Simeon', predicted his future greatness.[3]

Whether the resemblance between the stories of the two
great teachers has been heightened by borrowing between
their disciples of material congenial to feeling, or was due
to the fashioning of each tradition through feelings common

[1] Translation by Swami Prabhavananda and C. Isherwood, pp. 60-61.
[2] According to the philosophy of the *Gita* the incarnate God, unlike the
ordinary mortal, 'remains master of Prakriti, the bodily vehicle (see
Appendix, *op. cit.* pp. 179-180). He could not be conceived as subject, like
the Christ of the Gospels, in common with us, to the temptations and
agony of the flesh.
[3] Sir S. Radhakrishnan has discussed these parallels in *Eastern Religions and
Western Thought* (Oxford University Press), Ch. V, 2.

to men of different races telling of a revered master, we need not seek to decide. Our interest is in tracing these type-patterns—similarities in the thought and literature of different ages and races of men—related to the most universal conditions and attitudes of human life. Tracing the elements of such a pattern in the tradition of divine incarnation we are led farther back than the stories of Jesus or Gautama, of Rama or Krishna.

In each of these stories a victorious conflict is depicted. In perhaps the oldest of them, the story of Rama, a god takes birth that victory may be achieved over a demon harmful to gods and men; in the others the aim of the victory sought is more clearly of a spiritual character: 'to destroy the sin of the sinner', to rescue men from the bondage of ignorance, from the power of Satan. Of the oldest form of this tradition of conflict between a divine hero and an evil power we have no adequate record. It can be guessed at only from references in ancient literature to 'floating material' more ancient still, transmitted only orally. A myth of a divine conflict seems to have blended with the myth of a divine rebirth in that most ancient religious pattern to which reference has been already made. Human dependence on the power of the sun's rays, experience of the seasonal renewal of life, and of the sun's victory over darkness and cold, we infer as one common source of the earliest myths both of divine rebirth and of the god's victory over an embodiment of evil.

An embodiment of harmfulness rather than of evil we should perhaps call this antagonist of the god in the myth's earliest form. The enemy appears as a serpent or dragon. Dr. Rudolf Otto has written of an ancient god, afterwards superseded in the Indian pantheon, who is referred to in ancient Aryan literature as overcoming a 'demonic abomination in the form of a serpent-dragon'.[1] This monster Otto

[1] *The Kingdom of God and the Son of Man*, pp. 27-8.

describes as a 'numen of terror', but not at first embodying a spirit or principle of evil. This it becomes only in the religion of Iran, when the primordial conflict assumed the form of warfare between 'the holy spirit of deity' and an adversary of fundamentally opposite nature.[1]

In the Hebrew scriptures we find a similar development of the myth of a divine victory over a monster, serpent or dragon. In the study by Dr. W. O. E. Oesterley[2] of the evolution of the messianic idea, passages are collected from the Psalms and prophetic writings of the Old Testament that contain relics of the myth in its earliest form. The prophet Amos, for example, refers to a serpent at the bottom of the sea, obedient to Jahwe, a serpent that at God's command shall bite those that rebel against him. (Amos IX, 3.) Such a reference shows, Dr. Oesterley observes, the existence of floating myth-material that was 'matter of common knowledge', a story orally transmitted of the sub-jugation of a sea-monster by Jahwe.[3] In the Psalms we find references to the same conquest: *Thou breakest the heads of Leviathan. Thou hast broken Rahab in pieces.* (Psalm LXXIV, 14, LXXXIX, 10.) In the Hebrew as in the Aryan scriptures this mythical conflict becomes spiritualized. The monster em-bodying evil, at first probably 'in the sense of harm-doing,' became Satan, still in metaphor 'the old serpent', but embodying 'evil in the sense of wickedness', the great adversary of the righteous and holy God.[4]

In both Aryan and Jewish religion we find that with the later development of the myth goes reversal of beginning and end. The aboriginal conflict is transferred to the final epoch, or is therein to be completed. Thus Isaiah puts in the future the subjugation of the monster: *In that day the Lord, with his sore and great and strong sword, shall punish Leviathan, the piercing serpent, even Leviathan that crooked serpent,*

---

[1] *The Kingdom of God and the Son of Man*, pp. 27-8.
[2] *The Evolution of the Messianic Idea* (Pitman, 1908).
[3] *op. cit.* p. 48.   [4] *ibid.* p. 179.

and he shall slay the dragon that is in the sea. (Is. xxvii, 1.) For us these dim myths of conflict gain significance when we recognize their influence in recorded words of Jesus. An eminent historian[1] has spoken of the way in which recent historic study of Jewish apocalyptic literature has revolutionized our idea of the New Testament. Such a revolutionizing influence I have felt strongly in the historic study by Dr. Otto[2] of the idea of the Kingdom of God, traced from its earliest known form in Aryan and Iranian religion to its dominance in the thought of Jesus as recorded in the Gospels. Otto has shown how different lines of thought and imagery meet and blend in the apocalyptic literature of the Jews: the idea of a divine Lord and Kingdom, of a conflict, final victory, and judgement of men and angels; of a figure intermediary between God and man—a Son of Man, to whom should be given the throne and power of divine judgement. All these ideas, present in later apocalyptic writings—coming from sources part Aryan, part Hebrew—can be traced in the recorded teaching of Jesus.

Consider these passages, statement and prayer, quoted by Otto[3] from ancient Indian scriptures:

> A King over the entire world of existence
> He leads his kingdom to victory against all opposition.

This king is the all-wise Varuna. To him the prayer is offered:

> O that we
> In your far extended kingdom
> Which protects many, may be made one.

These passages show clearly two aspects of the divine

---

[1] F. M. Powicke in *Three Lectures* (Oxford University Press, 1947).
[2] A study carrying further the same influence felt in the work of Albert Schweitzer referred to above in the preceding essay.
[3] *The Kingdom of God and the Son of Man*, pp. 24, 25.

kingdom which appear in the teaching of Jesus. For the ancient Aryan worshipping more than a thousand years before Christ, as for Jesus of Nazareth, the divine kingdom was a unifying saving power to those who desired it, hostile and coercive towards evil forces opposing it.

I beheld Satan as lightning fall from Heaven, Jesus tells his disciples when they returned with joy because *the devils are subject unto us through thy name* (Luke x, 18). So also, the argument of Jesus against those who accused him of casting out devils through Beelzebub reveals, Otto urges, a conception 'of very ancient Aryan-Iranian origin', that of the divine kingdom as 'a realm of power', victorious over the realm or kingdom of evil. *If I, by the spirit of God cast out demons, then is the kingdom of God come unto you.* (Matt. xii, 28.) Luke's version of this saying, with its reference to Satan stripped of his armour (xi, 22) in Otto's view shows even more clearly the bearing of that vision of the fall of Satan: the spoil can be taken from the Evil One because he is already stripped of his power, his armour. The kingdom is inbreaking upon men as redeeming might and Jesus is aware of himself as its instrument.[1]

It is in the book of Enoch—in certain parts believed to have been written 94-64 B.C.—that passages occur most evidently influenced by Iranian thought and significant for their relation to recorded sayings of Jesus.

In the opening chapter there is reference to the divine conflict and victory: *the Great Holy One will march forth . . . with his hosts and in the strength of his power appear from heaven. Then will all fear. . . . The high mountains . . . will fall and pass away: the hills will sink and melt in the flame . . . and a judgement will take place over all.* (En. i, 3 ff.) The name used here, 'the Great Holy One', Otto regards as a translation of the term used of the Zoroastrian deity. It was among the

---

[1] Otto's interpretation of these passages concerning the opposing kingdoms is given in Book i, Part iv, Ch. 2 of *The Kingdom of God and the Son of Man.*

Aryans who passed into the Iranian plateau, and through the teaching of Zoroaster, that the ancient idea of a divine conflict acquired the profound meaning 'of the contest of the divine light with the demonic darkness of ungodliness'. The teaching, ethical and spiritual, of Zoroaster seems to have become on Iranian soil smothered under an accumulation of magic ritual before it gave place to the religion of Islam, but while it still lived it spread to other regions, quickening thought and aspiration.

In the Book of Daniel, where Persian influence is present, occurs the vision of one like unto the Son of Man to whom was given an everlasting dominion (vII, 14). In the *Similitudes* of Enoch the Son of Man appears more definitely as a superhuman being: *Before the sun and the signs of the Zodiac were created: his name was named before the Lord of Spirits*. These words might imply only existence in the ordaining and creative thought of God. Other sayings imply that the being thus named is in some manner already active: *For in him dwell . . . the spirit of instruction and of power and the spirit of those who have fallen asleep in righteousness.*[1] (En. xlix.)

Of this Son of Man it is also said: *the Most High kept him before his power, and the wisdom of the Lord of Spirits has revealed him to the holy and righteous ones*. Both these statements appear significant in relation to Jesus' thought of himself and the way in which he refused or permitted his thought to be revealed. While it was his own high consciousness of a mission that led Jesus, the carpenter's son, to identify himself with that Son of Man of whom the apocalyptic tradition told, it was not for Jesus himself, walking the earth in humility 'before his power', at once to inform men of his mystic relation to that one who should hereafter 'seat himself upon the throne of his glory'. (En. lxix.) When,

[1] We may compare here the Vedic teaching, not found in earlier Jewish writings, that the believer, escaping rebirth, enters at death into the spiritual body of his god.

however, at Caesarea Philippi, Peter to the question: *Whom say ye that I am?* answered: *Thou are the Christ*, Jesus could recognize the avowal as that revelation of the Son of Man which, according to prophesy, should be made by God to the righteous. Thereafter he could speak more freely of his foretold coming as the Son of Man enthroned in glory, when the Kingdom of God should break in upon the world within the lifetime, as he believed, of some of those who stood around him.[1]

Yet before that revelation of the Kingdom, the Son of Man had more to accomplish than the writers of the Book of Enoch knew—a sacrifice that only Jesus himself foresaw: *The Son of Man must suffer many things and be rejected and be killed. The Son of Man came to give his life a ransom for many.* The thought goes back clearly to the 53rd chapter of Isaiah: *He is despised and rejected . . . thou shalt make his soul an offering for sin.* By the time of Jesus it appears that, in the minds of many, the earlier conception of an earthly warrior-messiah had been synthesized with that of a supernatural judge and deliverer; but for the synthesis, effected in the thought of Jesus, of the deliverer, the Son of Man, with the suffering servant of Deutero-Isaiah there was no precedent. For this no one was prepared. Hence the violent repudiation and fear with which the disciples received Jesus' prediction of his sufferings and their dismay when the prediction was fulfilled.

Yet if there was no conscious acceptance by Jesus' disciples before his death, of the pattern in which the victor God is one with the slain victim, the redeeming sacrifice, that pattern, it has been shown, was present in the earliest gropings of human thought. 'The most fundamental idea',

[1] This instance of the interpretation by Otto of the Gospel record by reference to the Book of Enoch is given here because I find it both convincing and illustrative of historic continuity in the development of the idea of the divine entry into human life. Any reader concerned to question the validity of Otto's interpretation should, of course, refer to his own detailed exposition in the work cited.

says Professor Hooke,[1] speaking of the complete pattern of
the ancient religion, the idea of the dying and rising god,
was 'incompatible with the prophetic conception of Jahwe'.
Thus for a time that image was banished from the religious
thought of the devout Jew. Yet it was destined to return;
was operative, one would surmise, in the mystic ecstasy of
the writer of *Isaiah* LIII, as he told of the willing suffering
and death whereby atonement was made for the sin of
many. So also, the disciples meditating, after their Master's
death, on his teaching, could feel how deeply satisfying was
the completion through him of the underlying meaning of
the tradition of sacrifice: *Without shedding of blood is no
remission.* Not like every other High Priest's offering, a mere
figure of the true was that of Christ: *Now once in the end of the
world hath he appeared to put away sin by the sacrifice of himself.*
(Heb. IX, 22, 24, 26.)

What, we may ask, is the outcome—for our theme of a
birth, or inbreaking, of the Divine—of these historic researches into the teaching and influence of Jesus in relation
to the traditions he inherited?

First, we may note the different effect which historical
studies have on religious thought from that of research in
physical science. Studies that concentrate the mind on laws
of process in the material world may lead to sceptical
indifference towards the things of the spirit and the literature
in which these find expression. Studies equally searching
into the history of ideas do not diminish interest in religious
images, nor sense of their power, but may transform the
manner in which such images are held and their challenge
accepted.

If our minds respond to such historic studies as that of
Otto in regard to the life of Jesus, and if, at the same time,
we hold to the faith that the birth and ministry of Jesus

[1] In *The Age of Transition* (Sheldon Press, 1937), p. 263.

was indeed a coming into the world of the Divine, we must clothe our faith in forms somewhat different from those in which our Christian forefathers clothed theirs.

Necessarily, our whole thought of the life, teaching, and death of Jesus is thrown back into the image of his birth. One effect of Otto's interpretation—if we accept it—of the teaching of Jesus is that we shall think of his birth, as of his life, in his own terms rather than in those of the Christian Church. In Jesus' terms, that which broke in upon the world through his coming was God's Kingdom, a power of love, or spiritual fellowship, announced, and, in some indefinable way, embodied in him. Greater miracle was to come; the Kingdom in fullness of power was for the future to reveal; but at present its evidence, offered by Jesus, was his own mighty works, God's rescue of men through him from the power of Satan.

This work of healing and exorcism would be, according to our present-day thought, an arousing in the sufferers of those latent energies of mind and body that make for health. An influence over his fellow-men, unusual in its strength, calling forth such energies, must, we think, have been the source of the stories of healing and exorcism recorded in the Gospels. Such a saving healing power is not less a mystery, an inbreaking of the Divine, because we find analogies to it in other times and places.

Analogies to Jesus' acts of healing may be found among the many records of cures described as healing by faith. Of greater interest, I think, as analogous to that quickening sense of nearness of the Kingdom inspired by Jesus, are those later times when, through the influence of some person or group, full of hope and faith, to some minds a new age seemed dawning.

An analogy of this nature might be found in the influence over his fellows recorded of Gandhi at certain periods of his life. Of the spiritual exaltation of the time just before

G

the Bombay riots, C. F. Andrews has written: 'Things of great moment were being put right in a day such as in ordinary times would have taken generations to accomplish'. During 'a single visit of Mahatma Gandhi to Assam [a wave of public enthusiasm] swept away bad opium habits of half a century of addiction'. So, in regard to other evils: 'it seemed literally true, in those wonderful and inspiring days, that the age of miracles had returned'.[1]

Or one may think of those high hopes for his nation expressed by Milton in his *Areopagitica*: 'For now the time seems come when Moses, the great prophet may sit in heaven rejoicing to see that memorable and glorious wish of his fulfilled, when not only our seventy elders, but all the Lord's people, are become prophets'. 'Methinks I see in my mind a noble and puissant nation rousing herself like a strong man after sleep. . . . I see her as an eagle mewing her mighty youth and kindling her undazzled eyes at the full midday beam; purging and unsealing her long abused sight at the fountain itself of heavenly radiance.'

In all these times of eager expectation and sense of divine power operative in the world, there was an element of delusion. That return of the Son of Man in glory, expected within the span of a human life-time, did not happen. The exultation of Milton, and that of Gandhi, gave place to bitter disappointment. Yet in those times of ardent faith and aspiration we encounter something immortal, illumining the past and, like a beacon, shining into the future.

To the present writer it seems that our reverence for the Gospel story of the birth, ministry, and death of Jesus, as an entry of the Divine into our human order, is not diminished when, looking both forward and backward through the vistas of history, we recognize such entry as occurring not in one unique revelation only, but again and again, perceived under differing forms of imagery relative

[1] *Mahatma Gandhi's Ideas*, p. 277.

to the growth and change of other factors in the life of men.

From our thought of the Divine entry we may turn now to consider that other happening symbolized in Yeats' poem: the birth—the inbreaking or breaking out—of a force the opposite of the Divine Kingdom.

IV

The blood-dimmed tide is loosed; the best lack all conviction. After the depicting, in Yeats' poem, of horror and helplessness, comes the cry:

> Surely some revelation is at hand.
> Surely the Second Coming is at hand.

And then the image of the sphinx-like monster raising itself in the desert, a portent of something—contrary to hope—to be born into the world at Messiah's birthplace.

It is in the terms suggested by Yeats' poem that I shall speak of the calamities that have come upon us in two world-wars. My aim is not to give any account of these calamities or their causes; but to pursue the study of what I have termed the archetype of numinous birth by considering, in relation to what actually followed, that premonition of a coming birth or revelation that appeared in the writings of certain authors of the time, and, most powerfully, in the writings of Nietzsche.[1]

'Man is something to be surpassed.' 'I teach you the superman: he that is lightning, he that is frenzy.' 'Man is a rope stretched between the animal and the superman—a

---

[1] Here I speak of Nietzsche only. In *The Heritage of Symbolism* by C. M. Bowra (Macmillan, 1943) a study is made of certain other writers, notably Stefan George and Alexander Blok, in whose thought and poetry powerful images appeared foreshadowing the birth or revelation of a force or being answering to a need, and stirring religious devotion, in the poet and those to whom his influence extended.

rope over an abyss, a dangerous crossing, a dangerous wayfaring. What is great in man is that he is a bridge and not a goal.' 'One must still have chaos in one to give birth to a dancing star.'

These sayings from the Prologue of *Thus Spake Zarathustra* indicate some main features of Nietzsche's premonition and hope concerning the new birth. The superman to whose coming Nietzche looks forward is to be born of man, not of God, yet of that in man which is allied with the lightning and with the abyss, with frenzy and chaos. It is not from man as he is that Nietzsche's hope springs, but from that in man which has power to create, sending beyond itself 'the arrow of longing'. Nietzsche writes as a poet, accepting and enduring for the sake of creation the chaos within himself, the surging up within him of the troubled depths of good and evil. It is for the sake of creation that danger must be faced: danger in looking back, arousing vital energies of the brute, danger in looking forward with desire and love of the remote, the yet untried.

To me it seems that we best realize the meaning and value of Nietzsche's writings, especially in *Zarathustra*, when we think of him as a poet dominated by that dynamic idea he named the superman, but which I venture to term the archetype of numinous birth. The image Nietzsche offers of a star to be born of inner chaos and conflict, seems a true symbol of this domination. The star that is another world —to us, though unknown, fascinating in its shining lure— comes as near perhaps as imagery can to expressing the goal of that urge which is so deep a part of our nature towards the unknown future that we together with alien forces shall create.

Nietzsche's emotion in writing of the Superman his sister describes[1] as 'overpowering passion'. With this passionate

[1] In the Introduction contributed by Mrs. Förster-Nietzsche to *Thus Spake Zarathustra,* translated by Thomas Common (Allen & Unwin).

intensity the Superman is 'put before us as the aim of our life, hope and will'. Something of this emotion is communicated, I think, in certain passages of *Zarathustra*; for instance that which tells of 'the fervent creative will' impelled to man as to a stone in which an image slumbers. Against the imprisoning stone 'my hammer rageth ruthlessly'. The work must be completed, the image released; 'for a shadow came unto me—the stillest and lightest of all things once came unto me! The beauty of the Superman came unto me as a shadow. Ah my brethren! Of what account now are the Gods to me!' (XXIV.)

'To create', Nietzsche, as Zarathustra, declares, 'that is the great release from suffering, and life-alleviation. But for the creator to appear suffering is needed. . . . For the creator himself to be the new born child, he must be willing to be the child-bearer and endure the pangs of the child-bearer. Verily, through a hundred souls I went my way and through a hundred cradles and birth throes . . . all feeling suffereth in me and is in prison.' (XXIV.)

We can recognize here, I think, the authentic note of religious faith directed towards the future, a faith like that by which St. Paul knew himself crucified and reborn with Christ and beheld the whole creation waiting in travail for the manifestation of the sons of God. Other analogies with the Gospel teaching appear; as when Zarathustra warns his disciples against neighbour love that is not subordinated to the love that is creative, the love of the future: 'Higher than love to your neighbour is love to the furthest and future ones.' ' "Myself do I offer unto my love, and my neighbour as myself"—such is the language of all creators.' (XVI, XXV.) Even so did Jesus condemn the neighbour love that should stand in the way of love and service of the Kingdom: *If any man hate not his father and mother and wife and child and brethren and sisters yea and his own life also, he cannot be my disciple.* (Luke XIV, 26.)

Again, when Nietzsche uses the image of the child to express the joyous spontaneity of the freed creative spirit, we recall the teaching of Jesus and of St. Paul. 'Three metamorphoses do I designate to you', says Zarathustra in the opening passage after the Prologue, 'how the spirit becomes a camel, the camel a lion, and the lion at last a child.' The camel, the load-bearing spirit, patient and reverent, becomes a lion contending for freedom against established values; but the lion cannot create new values. For that the lion must become a child, 'a new beginning, a game, a self-rolling wheel, a first movement, a holy yea into life'. The load-bearing camel is an image such as St. Paul might have used of the spirit oppressed by that burden of the law from which the creature made new and free in Christ rejoices to be delivered. The young child was accepted by Jesus as an image of the attitude he desired in his disciples: *Of such is the Kingdom of God.*

Analogies such as these are to be expected in the spiritual teaching of different prophets if it is true that certain patterns, symbolizing the life of the spirit, characterize human imaginative thought, however mixed with delusion. What of the differences between Nietzsche's hope of a new birth and that contained in the Christian Gospel?

One great difference between Nietzsche's vision of the New Birth and that of the Christian Gospels is in the relation recognized to prior ethical tradition. In the joy and freedom of those new born in the spirit, Jesus and his followers expected fulfilment of that righteousness the law had in vain demanded. In the power of the age to come, of the divine Kingdom in some manner already present, the warfare long ago initiated against evil is to be carried on. Nietzsche, like Jesus and St. Paul, conceived the New Birth as freedom from bondage to ancient law, but he repudiated, with law's constraint, its ethical content also. When the spirit becomes a lion, willing freedom and lordship, its task is to overcome the dragon on whose scales 'glitter the already created values of a thousand years'. ' "Thou shalt" is the great dragon called.' In a later passage a reason is offered for the repudiation of restraining law. It is the same reason or cause as that hinted at in Yeats' poem for the birth of the beast. ' "Thou shalt not rob! Thou shalt not slay"—such precepts were once called holy; . . . Is there not even in all life —robbing and slaying? And for such precepts to be called holy, was not *truth* itself thereby slain? . . . O my brethren, break up, break up for me the old tables!' (LVI, 10.)

To Nietzsche's time belonged a new insight into the unceasing struggle within nature, the predatory character of animal life. Accepting the truth of this, Nietzsche shaped in accordance with it his human ideal. Into the new creation he felt there must flow freely the energies of animal life, the latent energies of the human body. Not, perhaps, into the original teaching of Jesus, but into the life and teaching of the Christian church, asceticism had entered. The cradle, and cross, of Christ became for a time symbols of a way of life that so frustrated natural impulse as truly, in Yeats' phrase, to 'vex to nightmare' the sleeping powers of the animal man. Those powers Nietzsche, as prophet of his generation, desired to liberate, though, in *Zarathustra*, he still recognized the danger incurred.

In a significant passage of the First Book, Zarathustra is confronted with a youth dismayed at the evil he finds in himself when he seeks to enjoy freedom. Zarathustra perceives that while the youth is seeking freedom, he is not yet free: 'for the stars thirsteth thy soul. But thy bad impulses also thirst for freedom. Thy wild dogs want liberty; they bark for joy in their cellar when thy spirit endeavoureth to open all prison doors. Still art thou a prisoner . . . To purify himself is still necessary for the freedman of the spirit. Much of the prison and the mould still remaineth in him.' (VIII.)

Not simply to free nor to subdue the brute impulses within oneself, but to purify and transform them, is the achievement of the New Birth; this Nietzsche had the insight to discern. Of that type of ascetic saint that he terms the Sublime One, solemn, penitent, self-engrossed, Zarathustra asserts he must unlearn his hero-will that has subdued monsters—the wild beasts that, yet unchanged, gaze out from his seriousness. 'He should also redeem his monsters . . . into heavenly children should he transform them.' (xxxv).

Yet how should this task of redemption be accomplished if the wisdom is rejected of all those who in the past have encountered the same problem? The hope that Nietzsche offered in the prophetic ecstasy that inspired *Zarathustra* was too empty of content for the purifying transforming work required of it.

In Nietzsche's later writings there seems evidence of increasing tension between the gentler and fiercer impulses of his nature; loss of insight also into all that the New Birth should mean. Violent reaction against Christian ethics and democratic ideals found expression in images of savage power-worship that correspond only too closely to horrors that have since become actual. 'Life is essentially appropriation, violation, the overpowering of the feeble and the strange; suppression, hardness, the forcible imposition of its own forms, mutual devouring or at least, to put it mildly, exploitation . . . precisely because life is Will to Power.'[1] When this 'basic factor in all history' is accepted as also the determinant of the moral ideal, it follows logically that Christian morality, with its teaching of compassion and of human equality before God, should be regarded as part of a 'slave insurrection' against natural rulers. The true 'master-morality' untainted by Christian influence was that of 'people who scorned "inclusion within the social pale"

[1] From *Beyond Good and Evil*.

that they themselves had created, and constantly slipped outside, back into the innocent conscience of the beast of prey, like exulting monsters who depart from an outrageous succession of murders, incendiaries, rapes and tortures, in high spirits as though it were only a students' rag.'[1] Here, as it seems, in hideous premonition emerges the image of that 'blonde beast' that has become so strongly associated with Nietzsche's name: the beast 'avidly rampant for spoil and victory' that he recognizes as existing at the core of all aristocratic races, inevitably from time to time finding outlet.

In the passage quoted Nietzsche speaks of slipping 'back into the innocent conscience of the beast of prey', but actually men cannot thus slip back. The horror of bestial cruelty in men of our time is in the conscious violation by them of insights a beast has not. The cruel Will to Power, regardless of other men's rights, that finds embodiment in a tyrannical ruler or fiercely dominant party or class, appears better symbolized not as the mere innocent beast of prey but as that numinous Birth of Yeats' poem: the shape lion-bodied with the head of a man.

Much speculation has centred about the sphinx image, as it appears in ancient art and myth. But indeed, the blending in a visible shape of human and animal qualities presents a symbol of far-reaching potentialities that may take, in new conditions, ever new meaning. That the monster of Yeats' vision is seen in the desert, stirring its slow thighs, links it with the strange, enduring sphinx-shape found there; links it perhaps also with that sinister desert-numen, Azazel, for whom—when lots had been drawn between him and Jahwe—the scapegoat thus chosen was sent into the wilderness. (Lev. xvi, R.V.) But the central meaning, in Yeats' poem, of the man-headed monster must be given in the line that tells how it slouches towards Messiah's birthplace to be born. It is in the soul of man,

---

[1] From *Genealogy of Morals*.

where might be born Christ, the new Adam, that a birth of
bestial savagery—sharpened by human intelligence, but
lacking human compassion, like a force of nature, 'pitiless
as the sun'—becomes numinous, a birth of evil transcending
nature.

A German writer who lived at close range through the
gathering force of the Nazi terror and the horrors of the war,
has recorded their effect on him: an impression so powerful,
of transcendent forces of evil, that he has come to interpret
all life and literature in terms of such forces and their
opposite. The greatest minds, he thinks, have recognized
not only divine power, but such forces as those for which
Shakespeare found expressive speech when he made Lady
Macbeth cry her summons:

> Come to my woman's breasts,
> And take my milk for gall, you murdering ministers,
> Wherever in your sightless substances
> You wait on nature's mischief . . .

In the Nazi terror, when previously quiet and seemingly
harmless people became ready to witness calmly or even
share in extremes of brutality, Alfred Weber felt, he says,
in such a sudden and terrible 'darkening of mind', 'the
uncanny wing-beat of those powers' whose effects historians
had described but which he had never appreciated as real
and capable of dominating his own people. 'The wing-
beat', he repeats, 'of the dark-daemonic forces; there is no
other term for their suprapersonal and transcendent power.'[1]

At the conclusion of this essay I wish to speak again of
the belief in transcendent forces both of evil and of good
that break into that known or familiar order we term
natural. Before touching on this belief and its relation to
the type-image of divine birth, I wish to illustrate something

[1] Alfred Weber in *Farewell to European History*, translated by R. F. C. Hull
(Kegan Paul, 1947.)

of the influence in later poetry of the image presented supremely in the Gospel story of the birth of Christ.

v

I have chosen, it may seem somewhat arbitrarily, a few poems to illustrate the use in poetry of images of incarnation. Other poems for other readers might express better such images in their power over thought and emotion. To justify choice, if it seem arbitrary, one can speak only of the inevitable limitation of every reader's encounter with poetry; each can receive, and attempt reflectively to communicate, only as resources of an individual life-history allow.

Milton's *Ode on the Morning of Christ's Nativity* I take as an instance—for me of distinctive value—of a poet's use of the image of Divine birth, at a time when the story as told in the Gospels was accepted as a supreme fact of history. By me, this poem, loved in childhood, was so accepted. It celebrated, I understood, an actual event, yet in terms so lovely and fantastic as to set it apart, infinitely remote though compelling, like some jewel-bright scene in the glass of a church window.

Strongest of all was the impression conveyed by the later verses of the poem, telling of the Old Dragon underground, lashing 'the scaly horror of his folded tail' in wrath at the failure of his kingdom, of the silenced oracles, the 'hollow shriek' of the god deserting his shrine, and grief of fairy presences dispossessed:

> The lonely mountains o'er
> And the resounding shore
>   A voice of weeping heard and loud lament;
> From haunted spring and dale
> Edg'd with poplar pale,
>   The parting Genius is with sighing sent.
> With flower-inwoven tresses torn
> The Nymphs in twilight shade of tangled thicket mourn.

There was for me something of death and terror in the
sense conveyed of a powerful magic in the Divine birth; in
those 'rays of Bethlehem' that could blind the eyes of
heathen gods.

> Our Babe, to show his Godhead true
> Can in his swaddling bands control the damned crew.

Here, I felt, was a fairy tale that could brook no other fairy
tales beside it, and made, moreover, demands upon one's
life those others did not make.

The impression of magic thus communicated gives one
perhaps a clue to something of what is experienced by adult
minds of a more primitive community to whom missionaries
bring the Gospel story. 'Our life was passed in fear of the
spirits. Now Christ has come and it is all different.' This,
Bishop Neill has said,[1] might be the account given by his
Tamil converts, on the first Christmas after their baptism,
of the change the Gospel message had brought to their
lives. To Milton, and to the child in the Victorian age
responding to his poem unquestioningly, the nymphs and
demons made impotent by the divine birth had little of that
malignant power the Tamil converts had known; but there
is something, surely, of the same troubling, dimly numinous
magic, felt by child and primitive alike in the imaged story
of this Birth, and all it wrought upon the world.

Beside these verses of Milton's poem, I would set a poem
by T. S. Eliot, as different in method as Milton's time and
ours are different, conveying also, though in terms of mystic
insight rather than of magic, an impression of death and
terror in the Divine birth.

In Eliot's poem, *Journey of the Magi*, the imagery is not
fantastic and remote but precise in its detail, the speech
almost that of every day:

[1] In *The Christian News-Letter*, 24 December 1947.

A cold coming we had of it,
Just the worst time of the year
For a journey and such a long journey:
The ways deep and the weather sharp,
The very dead of winter.

These words, adapted from Bishop Andrewes, presenting
the journey as though it might have happened yesterday,
set the tone for the other imagery of the poem:

> . . . the camels galled, sore-footed, refractory,
> Lying down in the melting snow.
>
> .   .   .   .
>
> And the villages dirty and charging high prices:

At the end, after the vivid matter-of-fact account of the
journey, come lines that tell of the enduring, mysterious
influence of the Birth at last encountered:

> . . . Were we led all that way for
> Birth or Death? There was a Birth certainly
> We had evidence and no doubt. I had seen birth and death,
> But had thought they were different; this Birth was
> Hard and bitter agony for us, like Death, our death.
> We returned to our places, these Kingdoms,
> But no longer at ease here in the old dispensation
> With an alien people clutching their gods.
> I should be glad of another death.

Is this agony, again, such as the Tamil converts might
have known when hours came of loneliness and misgiving,
torn between the new faith and the old beliefs of their
kinsfolk and their own childhood? That may be the first
meaning of the agony like death suffered by the star-guided
travellers. Yet there is another, more universal, meaning
in the lines. 'The time of death is every moment', T. S. Eliot
has written. In every moment is a beginning and an end.
Of every moment the Divine Birth that is also Death may

be a symbol, but a symbol most of all, of those moments
each of us, perhaps, has shared in some degree with poets
and prophets, when it seems that something is born to us,
divine, uncontaminated, as if it came from another world,
a hope and pledge of union between that world and ours.

Such a moment Nietzsche was perhaps recording when
he told of that still ecstasy in which there came to him 'the
beauty of the superman'. Of such a moment, it seems,
Rousseau was writing when he told how on the road from
Paris to Vincennes he saw, weeping, and dazzled by crowd-
ing ideas as by a thousand lights, all the contradictions of
the social system and that 'man is naturally good', and
what he might be in a society that could liberate in all men
that essence and desire of goodness.[1]

On Rousseau's vision, expounded in his writings and
accepted by many as expressing their own truth, there
followed, in part as a consequence, the French Revolution
with all its mixed good and evil. Of Nietzsche's rendering
of his vision of the Superman we think now as one influence
contributing to the orgy of death human passions have so
recently brought about. Must we then—the question
suggests itself—when we seek to incarnate a meaning that
seems divine be haunted by a premonition of death: death
of good that must be sacrificed in the pursuit of our purpose,
death of some finer meaning within the purpose itself,
violated in the struggle for its realization?

To me it seems that this is a condition of our human effort
that the Christian story of Divine birth and death helps us
to accept without despair. One other passage of contemporary poetry I quote here because I feel that it expresses

[1] In his *Confessions* Rousseau says of this moment that he 'beheld another
world and became another man', but forgot the details of his vision after
writing an account of it in a letter to M. de Malesherbes. What he could
retain of the vision he says was 'feebly scattered' in his three principal
writings; so that we may believe all he tried subsequently to say of the
'natural' education and 'natural' society appeared to him as glimpsed in
that moment.

with beauty and tenderness this aspect of the Divine Birth image: the mingling with its joy of a shadow of death and anguish.

In a work by W. H. Auden, entitled *For the Time Being, a Christmas Oratorio*, occur verses spoken 'at the Manger', a lullaby of Mary to her Babe:

> Sleep. What have you learned from the womb that bore you
> But an anxiety your Father cannot feel?
> Sleep. What will the flesh I gave you do for you,
> Or my mother love, but tempt you from His will?
> Why was I chosen to teach His Son to weep?
>   Little One sleep.
>
> Dream. In human dreams earth ascends to Heaven
> Where no one need pray nor ever feel alone.
> In your first few hours of life here, O have you
> Chosen already what death must be your own?
> How soon will you start on the Sorrowful Way?
>   Dream while you may.

Here, within the direct presentation of the Mother's foreboding for her divine child, one can feel the wider meaning symbolized: how with every divine thing entering our world mingles the heritage that dooms it to suffering and partial or apparent failure.

To Milton's *Nativity* Ode we may turn again to recall the thought traditionally linked with the image of Divine birth: the thought of a Golden Age imaged as both long past and to be renewed to man. In another poem Milton has told how solemn music could bring all Heaven before his eyes; so, in this *Ode*, the thought of the dawning Divine Kingdom is linked with that music of angels the shepherds heard. The dream of the angelic symphony, enwrapping fancy, can make time 'run back and fetch the age of gold'; then:

. . . leprous Sin will melt from earthly mould;
And Hell itself will pass away
And leave her dolorous mansions to the peering day.

The age of gold, here lightly sketched, with Truth and
Justice returning, rainbow orbed, to men, may remind us
of another poem telling of a birth, divine or half-divine,
bringing the golden age: a vision described with an antique
lightness of touch very different from the tragic seriousness of
the story of Jesus and his vision of the Kingdom. Strangely,
this poem, Virgil's Fourth Eclogue, was felt in the middle
ages as a direct prophesy of the birth of Christ.

'Thou didst light me on to God' Dante makes the poet
Statius relate to Virgil, when they meet in Purgatory.

> When thou saidst 'The world is renewed, justice
> returns and the first age of man and a new
> progeny descends from heaven'

the words so harmonized 'with the true belief sown by the
apostles of the everlasting kingdom' that the poet was led
to receive baptism and become, secretly, a Christian.

Yet Virgil's pastoral, however it may have been influenced
through his acquaintance with Jewish Sybilline prophesy,
has not the seriousness of the Jewish religious writings.
There must have been a playful spirit in the description of
a time when grapes shall hang on brambles, the earth
shower her gifts without cultivation, and the wool on sheep's
backs glow, conveniently, with colours suitable for human
robes of state. Likeness to Bible prophesy appears only in
the linking of this fantastic Eden with the birth of a child in
whose time the traces of bloodguiltiness shall be effaced and
the peoples released from age-long fear, while to him shall
be given 'life divine'.[1]

---

[1] *. . . si qua manent sceleris vestigia nostri,*
inrita perpetua solvent formidine terras.
ille deum vitam accipiet. . . .

Virgil's poem, telling of a golden age to be ushered in through a babe born to his patron and friend[1] may be thought of as the first recorded dream of many—written or perhaps unwritten—shaped in an imagination quickened by the birth of a desired child. Into such parental dreams the thought of the infant Christ may often enter.

Such a dream is that of Yeats, praying for his son, Michael, that he may be guarded from those who, like Herod of old, would seek to bring to nought that great 'deed or thought that waits upon his future days'. Into the prayer comes an expression of wonder—stirred one may guess by the father's sight of his babe's pitiful helplessness—at the Christian conception of divine incarnation:

> Though You can fashion everything
> From nothing every day and teach
> The morning stars to sing,
> You have lacked articulate speech
> To tell Your simplest wants, and known
> Wailing upon a woman's knee,
> All of that worst ignominy
> Of flesh and bone.

In Browning's poem, *The Ring and the Book,* two passages link the thought of the divine Babe with a human birth.

To the villain of the poem, the murderer Guido, lines are given describing—with a passion simulated with intent to touch the hearts of his judges—his thought of the coming birth of a son. The passionate description, though, within the drama of the poem, falsely uttered, yet seems drawn, by the poet who lends it, from deep sources of emotion.

That his wife, Pompilia, should have deserted him when a child was conceived put a brand, says Guido, on this first-born child:

---

[1] Scholars have failed to determine of whose child Virgil speaks, whether that of Pollio, or born—in Pollio's consulship—to a greater man. However this may be, the lines suggest, on the part of the poet, some degree of tender interest in the child.

H

The child I had died to see though in a dream,
The child I was bid strike out for, beat the wave
And baffle the tide of troubles where I swam,
So I might touch shore, lay down life at last
At the feet so dim and distant and divine
Of the apparition, as t'were Mary's Babe
Had held, through night and storm, the torch aloft—

Though the use of these words is given to the false Guido, it is Pompilia who hears in truth the summons to risk all, beat back the waves of trouble round her, for the sake of the coming child; and on her death-bed, when she looks back on the birth of her child at the holy time of Christmas, she has words for her thought linking the human with the Divine birth:

I never realized God's birth before—
How He grew likest God in being born.
This time I felt like Mary, had my babe
Lying a little on my breast like hers.

Strange contrast here to the thought of Yeats, the father shocked almost, by 'that worst ignominy of flesh and bone' the spirit suffers in the babe 'wailing upon a woman's knee!'

That same thought of ignominy suffered by the newly incarnate spirit appears in the lines Tennyson addressed to his infant son:

. . . O dear spirit half-lost
In thine own shadow and this fleshly sign
That thou are thou—who wailest, being born
And banished into mystery.

So, surely, we must conceive the spirit, lost or deeply veiled in the flesh of the helpless babe; yet Pompilia's phrase 'likest God', can express something of the truth of the human encounter with the Divine: how it is not in the object only, but between the *I* and *Thou* that the possibility of the encounter lies. To whatever the human spirit and flesh together respond profoundly, there is the encounter; and so the mother may meet God most truly in the helplessness of her new-born child, its veiled potentialities dependent on her fostering care.

Of one other poem I would speak that surveys every human birth as presenting the mystery of an incarnation. Wordsworth's *Ode on Intimations of Immortality* gives memorable expression to the Platonic thought of the spirit's pre-existence and fall from another sphere:

> Our birth is but a sleep and a forgetting:
> The soul that rises with us, our life's star,
>   Hath had elsewhere its setting,
>   And cometh from afar:
>   Not in entire forgetfulness,
>   And not in utter nakedness,
> But trailing clouds of glory do we come
>   From God, who is our home:

As in Plato's dialogue there rises in Socrates while he speaks 'a yearning for past happiness', when the spirit knew freedom from the body now imaged as its tomb or hard encasing shell,[1] so Wordsworth's poem images 'shades of the prison-house' closing in about the child as he grows to manhood, darkness falling on him and a weight of custom, while yet intimations remain, 'shadowy recollections' that can be through life an illuminating, sustaining power.

In any poem to which we respond with welcoming assent, or 'poetic faith', we can recognize, I think, both a distinctive outlook on the world, different from our own, which we can share only tentatively through imaginative sympathy, and also an element appearing more universal, the same to which Keats made reference when he wrote of poetry, 'it

[1] *Phaedrus.* 250.

should strike the reader as a wording of his own highest
thoughts and appear almost a remembrance'.[1] In Wordsworth's *Ode* a more individual factor is the insistence on the
visionary glory of the child's encounter with nature. Not
many readers can shape their image of childhood from
recollections of such a childhood as Wordsworth's. Yet
many of us, perhaps, recall moments of rapturous meeting
with the life and beauty of flowers, of moving water, of
changing light, memories that help us to conceive the ecstatic
communion of which Wordsworth tells. The later experience of 'moving about in worlds not realized', the haunting
by 'shadowy recollections' as of something once known that
both illumines and challenges all our present life: this, for
me at least, is an intimation, more convincing than any
recognized memory from childhood, of another sphere to
which our spirits are akin. Such intimations Plato thought
were native to humanity, though more present to some
minds than to others.

For no archetype, or shaping principle in thought or
imagination, can we, I think, claim more universality than
this: that it shall appear from age to age, powerfully,
creatively, in a few minds, awakening response in many.
So much we can claim for this belief, expressed by Plato and
by Wordsworth in imagery of the human spirit's prior
vision and fall at birth from heavenly places.

VI

'Belief expressed in imagery awakening response': in this
phrase I have attempted to describe that which in poetry
we term truth. We do not know how deeply or for how long
Wordsworth felt the imagery of his *Ode* to be an expression
of his personal belief. But the *Ode* has a quality of seriousness
and of passion that challenges belief. How fully a reader

[1] Letter to Taylor, his publisher, February 1818.

responds to this challenge, not merely entertaining the imagery as expressing the outlook of another mind, but appropriating it as an expression of his own, must depend upon his own resources and life history.

Every reader for whom poetry is an influence in his life finds, I think, certain poetic images which for him convey truth: truth not verifiable like the limited truths of science, but related to that wider truth or meaning that gives life value and purpose. For me one such image is Plato's picturing of the human spirit's fall from the heavenly vision, and recovery of it at moments and in glimpses through the wonder of mortal beauty and goodness. The vehicle of imagery is but a vehicle, whether it is the falling charioteer of Plato, or Wordsworth's 'trailing clouds of glory'. The creative impulse gladly fills out the detail of the picture or temporal drama by which essential meaning is conveyed. On this detail the affections fasten, especially when one has long lived with the image, meeting it and referring to it again and again. But it is some inner life of meaning—that thought may distinguish and, at a venture, put into conceptual terms, yet never wholly separate—that has illuminating power upon one's whole outlook, transforming power, even, on personality.

This distinction I would apply to that image of the Divine Birth presented in the Gospel story. Richly beautiful and dearly loved that imagery may become as one meets it again and again in poetry and pictorial art. As a possession of the heart and the imagination one would lose no detail of it: the annunciation to Mary, the angelic choir breaking in upon the shepherds in the darkened field, the wintry journey of the magi. Yet for some of us the impulse remains to seek from other sources a different clothing for the central meaning of this birth-story. The story tells of a divine power or being entering our world. Concerning this, historic research, and literary and philosophic comparisons, have something to reveal. Faith, in the sense of adherence of the whole personality, is given to that reality which is encountered through the aid alike of poetic imagery and of historic research and philosophic reflection.

We may ask what is our result if we apply this conclusion to that poem of Yeats which was our starting point.

In Yeats' poem—as in Wordsworth's *Ode* of such different quality—I recognize a challenging intensity, as though some powerfully conceived meaning shapes the course of the verse. I find that I give assent to that which the poem communicates. To tell myself in reflective speech what that communicated meaning is I have written this essay. It is of the universal tragedy that the poem speaks to me: how our world is entered by the Divine—perhaps, in eternity, once only, but for us again and again and always, as the eternal *now* is broken into our time-series, our *now* ever perishing and renewed—and again and again and always the divine thing is marred, obscured, so that, as time goes on, in place of it there seems to enter and arise its opposite.

Shall we assent to Alfred Weber's assertion, issuing from his terrible experience in Nazi Germany, that transcendent forces of evil, equally with those of good, can break into our world, maddening men, or winning their deliberate allegiance?

If I question my own belief—that interpretation of the world's evil conveyed through poetry and philosophy that I have found convincing—it does not appear that evil, though imaged personally, as Satan, God's great enemy, or as the 'rough beast' that can usurp Messiah's place, has the character of a birth from beyond—something transcendent entering our world—which belongs to our thought of the Divine.

That image of Satan which Jesus and the Gospel writers accepted from tradition to express their sense of the world's evil was descended from the ancient myth of a serpent or dragon, denizen of deep earth or sea. In Yeats' poem, although the sphinx-like monster approaches 'to be born', it is in the desert—some waste region of this earth—that it is seen rousing itself for its coming. Similarly, writers in a different speech medium, theoretic though imaginative,[1] seeking to express the force that invaded the minds of the German people, have named it Wotan, the ancient God who has lain hidden and breaks forth from some cavern or desolate northern region.

Thus, while, in imagery, the Divine descends from Heaven, it is from the earth that evil, serpent-like, arises. For the evil that persistently thwarts and defiles every earthly manifestation of the Divine we have another image in the clay, heavily resistant to the hand of the Divine potter. Of this image Yeats has given, in *The Countess Cathleen*, a vivid rendering:

> For surely He does not forsake the world,
> But stands before it modelling in the clay
> And moulding there His image. Age by age
> The clay wars with His fingers and pleads hard
> For its old heavy, dull and shapeless ease;
> But sometimes—though His hand is on it still—
> It moves awry and demon hordes are born.

The image of the resistant clay well expresses, I think, that element of pervasive evil in our world for which philosophers have sought some conceptual term. Plato has named it Necessity ($\dot{\alpha}\nu\dot{\alpha}\gamma\kappa\eta$) which Reason, the divine Artificer, over-rules, persuading it towards the best. He pictures it not as heavy, inert, but as flux, 'movement without order or harmony'. Whitehead, constructing his cosmic theory in the light of present-day research, accepts Plato's image as still valid, urging that into the 'physical agencies' conditioning the values that are possible such an element must enter, not derived from God.

[1] C. G. Jung in an article, 'Wotan', published 1936, included in *Essays on Contemporary Events* (Kegan Paul, 1947); also H. G. Baynes in *Germany Possessed* (Cape, 1941).

If with the man-headed monster of Yeats' vision we connect thoughts such as these concerning the evil element in the world, it will be the recalcitrance of the clay, the *urgrund* of the created world, that, as brutishness within our human nature, becomes devilish through the power lent it by an enslaved Reason. This, it seems to me, we may conceive as the essential being of the monstrous birth imaged in Yeats' poem.

One other image I take from Yeats to close this essay. It has been said of Yeats that he is 'a magical poet who has found a way of arranging concrete symbols that shall awake in us huge shadows of our wonder'.[1] One line from Yeats' short poem, *The Magi*, seems to me to have pre-eminently that power, giving form, as it were in vast concentric waves or shadows of meaning, to our wonder at the birth of the Divine into our troubled world.

'In the blue depth of the sky' appear to the poet those eternal travellers who ever seek—

> The uncontrollable mystery on the bestial floor.

In this strange line 'the bestial floor' may suggest, in first intention, the stable with its tethered oxen. Yet these, in our traditional image, are mild-eyed, companionable. Rather, the bestial floor is the whole world with its violence and obduracy. The uncontrollable mystery is that which the birth of Christ has come to mean through the experience of ages: that which, resisted, slain 'from the foundation of the world', by brutish violence, cannot be so vanquished. In our image of His birth we are aware also of His suffering and death and resurrection, the mystery of the Divine for ever entering the world, for ever obscured, destroyed, yet uncontrollably rising anew.

By L. A. G. Strong: quoted in *Th ePoetry of W. B. Yeats*, by Louis MacNeice (Oxford University Press, 1941), p .138.

III

THE SAGE, THE IMAGE OF WISDOM

O SAPIENTIA, quae ex ore Altissimi prodisti, attingens a fine usque ad finem fortiter, suaviterque disponens omnia: veni ad docendum nos viam prudentiae.

> An aged man is but a paltry thing,
> A tattered coat upon a stick, unless
> Soul clap its hands and sing, and louder sing
> For every tatter in its mortal dress,
> Nor is there singing school but studying
> Monuments of its own magnificence;
> And therefore I have sailed the seas and come
> To the holy city of Byzantium.
>
> O sages standing in God's holy fire
> As in the gold mosaic of a wall,
> Come from the holy fire, perne in a gyre,
> And be the singing masters of my soul.
> Consume my heart away; sick with desire
> And fastened to a dying animal
> It knows not what it is; and gather me
> Into the artifice of eternity.
>
> From *Sailing to Byzantium*.

Whomsoever the Muses, the daughters of Zeus, see fit to honour, beholding him sprung from the loins of Zeus-born kings, upon his tongue they pour sweet dew, and forth from his mouth flow honey-sweet words: upon him all the people gaze as he gives binding decisions, clear and just. This man, with his knowledge and with sureness of speech, can abate in a moment even the mightiest contention. For to this end were kings granted wisdom, that they might bring redress in the market-place to men of the people who suffer wrong, quietly and easily, persuading them with gentle words.

Hesiod, *Theog.*

THE intention of this essay is to examine, in relation to the human need that has shaped them, images of wisdom as they appear in imaginative and religious writings. Also we may follow a little way the track of this need for a type or representative of saving wisdom, as it finds expression in human institutions—life as studied by the historian and sociologist. The three poetic passages that I have placed before my essay may serve as points of reference, suggesting different aspects of the type-image.

The ancient prayer that generations of worshippers have chanted invokes wisdom conceived as divine, in its fullness beyond our conceiving but humbling itself to become our way of prudence, or understanding. The other two passages give further indication of the nature of the need the prayer expresses: need for understanding of human life both in its individual course and in the complex relations that arise between individual lives in a society. Also distinctive images are offered of the wisdom sought, incarnate in human life.

In the poem by Yeats, the need for some understanding of the individual life is made acute by an old man's sense of its transience. Not transience only; an element of futility, of mockery, is felt in life apart from some claim the spirit makes upon a power beyond it:

> An aged man is but a paltry thing,
> A tattered coat upon a stick, unless . . .

To establish its claim the spirit turns to 'monuments of its own magnificence'. The image of wisdom that could give meaning to life appears in the form of 'sages standing in God's holy fire as in the gold mosaic of a wall'. Such saints whose spirits soared, like the upward circling falcon—'perne in a gyre'—could teach the poet's spirit to aspire and rejoice amid the humiliations of bodily decay.

'Gather me into the artifice of eternity.' The strange phrase indicates the distinctive character of the poet's vision and prayer. The work of art, timeless in beauty, even as subject to time outlasting the generations of men, stands as the best symbol to the poet of eternity, and of that wisdom which, operating in human life and achievement, links it with the divine.

In our quest for the type-image of wisdom we may take account of the suggested claim of great art to embody a wisdom of special relevance to the spirit's need. But Yeats' poem offers a clue perhaps more essential in its expression of the need that prompts prayer to a Wisdom beyond even art's picturing. It is to the sages themselves that prayer is addressed: sages not held, like their material images, within the mosaic of the Byzantine artist, but coming from God's holy fire to work within a human spirit in its present suffering:

> Consume my heart away; sick with desire
> And fastened to a dying animal
> It knows not what it is;

Such bewilderment may assail most powerfully the spirit of the aged man. Yet not in age alone, at any moment in its mortal course, the human spirit may be pierced by a sense of the terrible incongruity between the vast range of vision that allures and longing that haunts it and the limitation, the animal needs and frustrations, of its bodily vehicle.

Here then is one suggestion, in the verse of a modern poet, of the nature of the need turning men from the transitory material world towards ideas and images conceived as mediating the spiritual, the eternal. We may look back through ancient and more recent records, questioning what evidence we find of such images haunting the human mind.

The lines quoted from Hesiod suggest a different aspect of the need for wisdom. The wisdom venerated is still conceived as divine. Hesiod's local kings, or city elders, are descended from Zeus; and the Muses, daughters of Zeus, have bestowed on them their gift of discernment and persuasive eloquence. Yet this divine gift is exercised amid the intricacies of social life, earthly affairs and interests.

A present-day sociologist[1] has undertaken elaborate studies of different cultures, based upon a distinction he believes illuminating, having reference to the main direction of attention within the culture—whether it is towards material or spiritual reality. There are difficulties in regard to such a distinction which we may consider later, but may take it here as characterizing the contrasted aspects of the image of wisdom.[2] The wisdom Hesiod praises is directed towards material reality, the transient life of the senses and bodily activities. This aspect of the image of wisdom we may also study in poetic and historic records and in our own experience, considering this need the image expresses and its relation to that other need that looks beyond the transient to the eternal.

Our hypothesis, here as elsewhere in these studies, is that by questioning our own response to records of human feeling objectified in imagery we may come to fuller understanding of our own nature in relation to the reality we encounter.

[1] Professor P. A. Sorokin in *Social and Cultural Dynamics* (first published in U.S.A.; republished, London, 1937).
[2] In speaking of 'the type-image of wisdom'—instead of always collectively of the imagery we study—I imply no more here than that we are seeking something common to the diverse imagery under which wisdom is conceived, or realized under human limitation. I would refer to that 'felicitous' account, which J. S. Mill in his *System of Logic* quotes from Whewell, of a group distinguished 'by Type not by definition'. A group having a Type for its 'director' is said to be 'determined not by a boundary line without, but by a central point within, not by what it strictly excludes but by what it eminently includes'. The different images here offered and discussed may be thought of as various approximations to such a central point. Further indication will be attempted later of what is meant by the terms 'type image' and 'archetype'.

II

'O Wisdom which camest out of the mouth of the most High . . . come and show us the way of understanding, Come, Lord Jesus.' The last words, added by the makers of the Free Church anthem book to their translation of the ancient Christian prayer, make explicit its intention. To Christian faith the supreme image of the divine wisdom that could guide and satisfy the human soul is found in the figure of the Jewish prophet and teacher that to the secular historian remains so enigmatic.

The Word was God . . . He was in the world and the world was made through him and the world knew him not . . . But as many as received him to them gave he power to become the sons of God. These assertions in the Prologue to St. John's Gospel focus the mystery of this Christian faith, bringing together the image of the obscure human life in Palestine, the slowly evolved thought of Hebrew prophets and Greek philosophers concerning the Divine Word, or Logos, mediating between God and man, and finally, the experience of those who found that this last of the Jewish prophets, Jesus, through his life and death and teaching had established for them a new and nearer relationship with God.

When we seek to realize, so far as for us is possible, the image the Fourth Gospel presents of divine wisdom incarnate in a human figure, help comes to us through the work of scholars tracing some of the sources of the distinctive ideal offered. The words of the sacred writings, familiar from childhood, become dulled, or if not dulled yet laden with associations we know to be alien from the experience originally communicated. Seeking to put ourselves back into that experience—of the circle of Christian disciples for and amongst whom the Johannine Gospel was written—we question what can be discovered concerning both the author himself and the outlook he had in common with those for whom he wrote.

Concerning the author the problem has been debated whether or not he was the Apostle John of whom the synoptic gospels speak; whether the assertion, 'the Word became flesh and dwelt among us and we beheld his glory', describes an encounter through physical sense or through purely spiritual vision. I myself find convincing that interpretation of the Fourth Gospel that attributes its assurance to the sense of relation with the Christ of inner experience, rather than to direct contact with the historic Jesus. The writer seems to have been one for whom the reported acts and words of Jesus had become momentous happenings within his own spirit and life.

Scholars have taught us to think of this writer whom we call St. John as a cultured Jew acquainted both with the Hebrew scriptures and with Greek philosophy. From the Old Testament and later Jewish writings he, and many of those for whom he wrote, had learnt to think of the divine Word as a creative energy present within the universe and inspiring the utterance of seers and prophets. In the writings of Greek philosophers they had found the idea of the Logos as creative reason, conceived more impersonally than by Jewish writers, yet still a divine energy, akin to reason in man, though infinitely beyond human reason in range and power.

The Greeks at Ephesus who had listened to the teaching of St. Paul would have received the story of the death and resurrection of Jesus into minds prepared by the mystery religions to welcome a saviour-god who died and rose again for man's deliverance. Yet no mystery religion ever fashioned a figure so firmly stationed in time and place as the Jesus of the Fourth Gospel; nor does the teaching of St. Paul, as we know it, present so vivid a picture. The writer we name St. John may have had personal contact with John, the Apostle, or some other who knew the historic Jesus. The writer's own power of mystic vision achieved the synthesis and transfigured realization of what he had learned from others.

That the vividly human figure who walked the dusty roads of Palestine in weariness and knew hunger and thirst, should have shared the omnipotence of God, having power over the elements and insight into the secret thoughts of men, would have been, we conceive, to the writer and first readers of St. John's Gospel, less hard to believe than it is to us. Before we can enter imaginatively the experience the gospel-writer sought to convey, we know that we should banish from our minds doubts suggested by the scientific and historic researches of our time. Whether the account given of the words and acts of Jesus has truth as we understand scientific and historic truth is a question with which St. John could not be concerned. His identification of the human figure of Jesus with the eternal Christ of the inner encounter appears unquestioning, and unquestioningly we can imaginatively accept it, postponing questions made necessary by the historic standards of to-day. Then we may perhaps experience, if faintly, something of what that figure of the Christ, human and divine, meant to the writer of the Gospel.

'We beheld his glory' St. John reports when at the marriage in Cana water is made wine, and imaginatively we can reach out towards the glory by which in the writer's experience the Christ has transfigured life—a glory of spiritual joy of which the elation of wine may serve as an imperfect symbol. So also, the restoring of sight for the blind, and of life to a physical form already corrupt in death, is felt both as sensible fact in the past and as present reality—the wonder of vision after blindness and new life from the dead brought to the spirit through its encounter with the Divine.

Thus the image of wisdom offered pre-eminently in St. John's Gospel is that of divine power and insight incarnate in a human life, freely communicable to those who can open heart and mind to its influence. Wisdom proceeding from the Most High that can rightly order all created things, in St. John's faith did once as the human Jesus, and can continuously as the eternal Christ, teach both the way of understanding and the joy of the spirit—become, in the words of Yeats' prayer to the glorified sages, the singing-master of the soul.

Between the experience of which St. John writes and the outlook of our own time runs a thread of historic relation. If we have studied, however inadequately, the tract of European history between the beginning of our era and our own day, we have become familiar with the influence of the Christian gospel as the New Testament writers shaped it, changing in form yet present continuously. So continuously that those of us who cannot identify as St. John did the divine Wisdom, the Logos, with the historic Jesus may feel we can both understand something of the process of change, and share in a central meaning that remains unchanged. Such historic continuity is for us Westerners lacking when we grope among the writings scholars have translated for us, expressing the image of wisdom formed by seers and thinkers of the Far East, in centuries before the birth of Christ.

Among Eastern sages claiming to communicate saving wisdom the figure that stands out most clearly is Gautama, the Buddha. The early accounts of his life make no claim for him of actual divinity; and of his supposed sayings we have abundant record. The difficulty that confronts us is in their interpretation. The question that for me rises most persistently, as I read the story and recorded sayings of the Buddha, concerns the reason of their persuasiveness: what was the relation of common feeling and presupposition between teacher and hearers that made possible glad acceptance of his doctrine?

We are told that when the Buddha had attained

enlightenment—after the long period during which, under 'the tree of wisdom', he enjoyed 'the bliss of emancipation', and after his surrender of that bliss, through the 'compassion for sentient beings' that drove him forth to preach 'the wonder-working truth'—he met first with five former companions, ascetics who, like himself dissatisfied with household life, had set forth as wanderers in search of wisdom and freedom. To these ascetics Gautama announced his discovery of the uselessness of such austerities as he and they had practised. He expounded the 'middle path' between extreme ascetism and the sensual life—'a path which opens the eyes and bestows understanding, which leads to peace of mind, to the higher wisdom, to full enlightenment, to Nirvana'. This is 'the noble eightfold path of right views, right aspirations, right speech, right conduct, right livelihood, right effort, right mindfulness, right rapture or contemplation'.[1]

When his first teaching had been accepted by the five ascetics, the Buddha further expounded to them the four Noble Truths: the truths concerning suffering and its origin, that it springs from craving, from attachment—in Rhys Davids' paraphrase 'from the conditions of individuality'—the truth concerning the passing away of suffering, that it is attained by no longer harbouring passion or craving; the truth concerning the way that leads to the destruction of suffering, that noble eightfold Path, already proclaimed'.

Of this teaching the supreme message is emancipation. In words ascribed to the Buddha, 'as the great ocean has one taste only, the taste of salt; just so have this doctrine and discipline but one flavour only, the flavour of emancipation'.[2]

Following upon the first conversions, many others, both men and women, welcomed the Buddha's teaching, some

[1] For this summary of the Buddha's teaching I have used the translation given by T. W. Rhys Davids, *Buddhist Suttas* (Oxford, 1900) and *Early Buddhism* (Constable, 1908).
[2] *Vinaya* I, 239.

becoming members of a religious order, accompanying the Buddha's wanderings, or going forth to spread his doctrine, others continuing their household life while practising the discipline so far as possible.

Again and again in Buddhist writings, as we read of the setting forth of the austere doctrine of emancipation, we find exultation expressed: the hearers 'glad at heart exalted the words of the Blessed One'. We, if we assent to the truths proclaimed by the Buddha, that all instinctive desires involve suffering, and that suffering may be escaped through renunciation, can hardly find in such teaching cause of ardent rejoicing. Did these early converts find in the doctrine implications that we miss, a positive element that the Noble Truths fail to make explicit?

What of the doctrine of Nirvana, as a goal of value far beyond the transient goods renounced by the Buddhist disciple? A recorded saying of the Buddha tells of his aim when he first went forth, renouncing the joys of his earlier life; he describes his dissatisfaction with that life, his dismay at the human condition subject to old age, disease, death and re-birth. Subject to these things it seemed wisdom to seek after that which is not subject thereto, even the supreme bliss and security of Nirvana.[1] This passage, and others that speak of Nirvana, suggest an intuition, such as seems common to mystics of all religions, of timeless blissful being of which all pictured heavens are sensuous symbols. Such an intuition imparted to responsive listeners by a teacher of 'numinous' personality, might, we can conceive, bring joy.

Yet a scholar of our own time who has made a life-study of ancient Buddhist writings denies the presence in the Buddha's teaching of any intuition of immortality. 'In the forefront of Buddhist exposition' says Rhys Davids, is put the 'impermanence of the individual soul', the complete rejection of all current soul-theories.[2] That the Buddha

---

[1] *Majjhima*, I, 163. [2] *Early Buddhism*, pp. 56-8.

should have rejected current theories of the soul's con-
tinuance we can well understand. We learn that at the time
in India souls of men and of all living things were thought
of as escaping at death from the bodies they had inhabited,
subtly material entities still subject to instinctive desires and
passions. If we understand the Buddha's assurance of the
impermanence of the soul to refer to such souls as these, his
teaching need not be held to deny to the self some other
mode of immortality. But in the view of Rhys Davids the
denial is absolute. The position of primitive Buddhism, he
observes, is so opposed to what is usually understood as
religious belief 'that there is great temptation to attempt to
find a loophole' through which in some way a soul and
future life can be recognized; 'there is no loophole'.[1]

Who or what, then, we may ask, achieves emancipation,
or, hoping for such emancipation, looks back and forward
to past and possible future lives, and follows the path that
leads, first to assurance of no rebirth 'to a state of woe',
and finally to knowledge that the possibility of rebirth is
utterly destroyed?[2] When the Buddhist teacher tells his
hearers of this path of emancipation, saying 'I have attained,
thou also canst attain, insight into past lives, assurance of
no future rebirth', is there not here implication of an
I and *Thou*, whose being is quite other than that of the
soul-entity of current picturing? Of the *I* and *Thou*, and
their relation, so deeply implicated in all our thought,
philosophers of the present day are struggling to realize the
significance and to find words for the expression; though
our common thought and speech seem ill-fitted for the task.
Deep and permanent in Indian thought has been awareness
in some manner of an *I*, an ultimate ground of being within
the self, and of an identity—of which the saint can become
aware—of this *I* with the supreme reality. That awareness,

[1] Introduction to the *Mahali Sutta, Dialogues of the Buddha* (Oxford, 1899
[2] These successive assurances are described in Suttas telling of the stages of
the Way.

we may conjecture, could persist when purified of illusion concerning a subtly material soul, and persisting could help to make possible communication between the Buddhist teacher and his hearer, with joy and sense of fulfilment in acceptance of the teaching.

I have dwelt on this point because it seems to me fundamental in the relation both of the Buddha to his immediate followers and of later teachers to their converts. The saint's challenge to discipline of bodily impulse, if it is to be in any measure effective, cannot be merely negative. It must meet in the hearer the response of some deep need. This need, met by the great ascetic religions of the East, is, I believe, no mere by-product of sexuality, as Freudian psychologists, terming it masochism, would have us believe. It is related, I would urge, to the part of our nature that we term spirit, which demands a goal not subject to time and death.

It is true that moments of spiritual realization are hard to attain. If we fail, or relax the effort, to strain thought and speech beyond their everyday temporal reference, we speak almost inevitably of the timeless joy of the spirit as a continuing beyond death into some other imaginable setting which the fulfilled desires of the body can enter. Yet when we so speak we know the heaven we picture is but a symbol. So, when disciples of the Buddha in later times speak of 'heaven' and 'another world', though they perhaps ignore the Buddha's warnings against superstitious sensuous hopes, they do not, I think, simply belie his essential teaching.[1]

'His majesty thinks nothing of much importance save what concerns the next world.' These words translate a sentence which the great Buddhist Emperor of India, Asoka, in the third century B.C. caused to be inscribed on rock for the instruction of his subjects.

These rock inscriptions are a monument, unlike any other

We may compare the way in which eternal life, in the Christian Scriptures, is both freely imaged as a future fulfilment and conceived as a present possession.

in the world, to an achievement of Buddhist teaching: the conversion of a warrior king in the midst of his career of conquest. 'His majesty feels remorse', Rock Edict XIII tells us, on account of the sufferings caused by his great victory in the ninth year of his reign over the Kalingas. His majesty now recognizes, the edict continues, as the chiefest conquest that of the Law of Piety (the Dhamma) which 'avails both for this world and the next'.

The terms in which the Emperor records his faith sound naïve and trite to us in the translation offered. It would be different perhaps if we could feel the meaning the sentences held for the mind that formulated them. Did Asoka, I wonder, image the next world of which he speaks as a place of subtly material pleasures? Or was he only expressing, as best he might, faith in a mode of being for which he knew no words he could find were adequate?

Before passing to speak of the teaching of other less distinct figures among Eastern sages, I should like to refer to a rendering of the story of the Buddha by a writer of our own time, the late Edward Thompson. In *The Youngest Disciple* (Faber, 1938), Edward Thompson offered an imaginative answer to the question I have found insistent, concerning the relation between the sage and his immediate followers.

The picture with which the story opens—of the Buddha appearing at the entrance of their forest cave to a band of robbers and two captive herd boys—well conveys the impression of a personality having that 'numinous' power which appears of special significance in the relation of the Eastern sage, or saint, to his disciples.[1] In the ancient narratives of the Buddha's life there are references to his majesty of bearing, 'calm and self-possessed', 'full of outward signs of worth'. But in the speech of our own day a portrait

[1] See the discussion by Rudolf Otto of the 'Holy Man', experienced by devotees as belonging 'to the side of the numen'. *The Idea of the Holy*, p. 162.

can be painted that in some ways speaks more effectively
to our imagination. Edward Thompson's story depicts the
awe of savage men at this visitant who appears as from
another world, having passed in tranquillity and utter fear-
lessness through the forest night where wild beasts hunted
their prey. His glance, commanding and 'quiet with pity'
subdues these brigands, and after speech that makes them
conscious of their evil deeds as pursuing them more relent-
lessly than any savage beast, he calls forth the two, robber
chief and herd boy, whom his insight has marked as future
disciples.

The imaginative rendering throughout the narrative of
the Buddha's relation, compassionate and austere, to those
who follow him, helps to give fuller meaning to the words,
repeated in slightly varying form, here as in the recorded
ancient dialogues, by those entering on discipleship: 'I take
refuge in the Blessed One, in the Truth, in the Order'.
Such 'refuge', according to the Buddha's recorded sayings,
can be found first in himself, as one who teaches and lives
the Truth, or the Law (Dhamma); later in that truth
recognized within the disciple's self. 'Look not for refuge
in any other', the Buddha urges in his last discourse:
'Holding fast to the truth, be to yourself a refuge'.[1]

In later vicissitudes of the Buddhist faith conveyed to
other lands, the human need of a religious refuge took
forms other than those the Buddha could have sanctioned.
In the Mahayana Buddhism of China and Japan, as in
medieval Christianity, the idea arose that 'merit', pertaining
to a divine or saintly life, could be transferred from saint to
sinner, like a charm or magic gift; and in their temples
Buddhist worshippers sought the favour of a figure personi-
fying not the wisdom of the Buddha but his compassion.

Other minds, however, among those influenced in these
lands by Buddhist teaching, carried on the quest for wisdom,

[1] 'The Book of the Great Decease', *Buddhist Suttas* (Oxford, 1900).

saving insight. One such was Lü Yen, a Chinese sage of the
eighth century A.D. Of his teaching an account is given in
a work translated, with introduction, by Richard Wilhelm,
entitled in English, *The Secret of the Golden Flower*.[1]

I have chosen to speak of the image of wisdom presented
in Lü Yen's teaching, partly because of the commentary
written on this teaching by Dr. Jung: a commentary motived
by an interest to which mine is similar, the interest in finding
in Eastern forms of thought psychological trends corresponding to those in minds he has studied in Europe.

Lü Yen's teaching—based upon the mystic doctrine of the
Tao, the Way, as expounded centuries before, in the Tao
Te Ching[2]—represented, Wilhelm writes, a reform of
degenerate Taoism. Like the Buddha, Lü Yen desired to
free men's minds from illusion, but unlike the Buddha, was
concerned explicitly with that element in the nature of man
that we term soul or spirit, and the question of its destiny
beyond death. Lü Yen recognizes in man two opposite
principles, one active, akin to the principle of light in the
natural world, the other dark, earth-bound. In a life
directed mainly towards external things, the earth-soul, he
taught, has mastery, and the ego thus dominated becomes
after death an impotent phantom, that enters soon upon
another life determined by its earthly memories. If, on the
other hand, release is attained from external things, the
light-principle becomes dominant and there is formed 'a
centre of life independent of bodily existence'. The being
thus freed can exercise after death an influence for good on
its fellows still in the flesh. At the highest stage, termed that
of the Golden Flower, the spirit returns to 'the undivided

[1] Translated from the German of Wilhelm into English by Cary Baynes,
with commentary by C. G. Jung (Kegan Paul, 1938).
[2] The book known as the Tao Te Ching, dated by Arthur Waley about
240 B..C is generally ascribed to Lao Tzu, though, according to Waley,
this is only the customary ascription to a 'legendary worthy', not implying
his actual authorship. See *The Way and its Power*, by A. Waley (Allen &
Unwin, 1934).

One, Tao', where is preserved 'in a transfigured form the idea of the person, the "traces" left by experience'.[1]

Such an account of man's nature as Lü Yen offers, involving a struggle of opposites, is congenial to the psychological thought of Jung. His own study of the human life-span has led him similarly to conceive of two opposite principles, one earth-born, emotional, instinctive, 'reaching far back into the depths of time and into the roots of physiological continuity'. In youth and early middle age, he holds, the instinctive desires and ambitions pertaining to this part of man's nature should be fulfilled. From such desires a certain release is necessary in the latter half of life, when the opposite principle we term spiritual should come more fully into play. It has long been part of the wisdom of the East that men and women growing old should, by a discipline of detachment, prepare their spirits for death. By some such discipline we too, Jung believes, may release a spiritual function neglect of which can cause both inward frustration and bodily disease.

It is the same intuition, stated by Jung in terms of his medical psychology, that Yeats has expressed in terms of poetry: 'An aged man is but a paltry thing, A tattered coat upon a stick, unless . . .'—an intuition welcomed perhaps more readily in poetry than when couched in language that may excite distrust as pseudo-scientific, lacking the definiteness we demand of scientific theory.

It is hard to relate adequately to our more exact knowledge the intuitions of moral and religious experience; yet

---

[1] It is of interest that this Chinese sage, unlike the thinkers of India, has conceived the final consummation in eternity as preserving some result of the temporal, earthly struggle. One may compare the thought of Professor Whitehead, that the divine nature both acts upon and receives reaction from the temporal world. So, the person who, in time, is but 'a route of occasions' may become in God, an ever present reality. (*Process and Reality*, Part V, Ch. II.) Though such transmutation is beyond our understanding, for many Western, if not for Eastern, thinkers, temporal life seems to have meaning only if something achieved through its struggle can pass into eternity.

by ignoring these we perhaps do greater violence to truth and to ourselves than by the most imperfect synthesis. In the brief discussion here offered of the records of great teachers, viewed in relation to present-day thought and need, I have suggested that their witness to man's relation with the eternal may remain valid in spite of differences of outlook between present and past. While we seek to enter imaginatively the complete experience communicated, we take into our own lives that which for us has unchanging truth. Of the existence of such truth, or relevance to human need, the power of these records to win response through the ages is our strongest evidence. As one illustration or fragment of such evidence, I have suggested the agreement with ancient teaching of the experience of a present-day medical psychologist.

The need expressed in Yeats' poem, recognized by the present-day psychologist, and communicated by the undying scriptures of the past, is that of the finite creature, man, for relation with the infinite, the eternal. But man has other needs. While this spiritual need shaped the ideal presented by the prophet-sages of past times, those times had other leaders, warrior-kings and statesmen-priests, who represented a different type of wisdom. We may continue our study by comparing with the image of the prophet that of the kingly leader whose wisdom includes more concern with the needs of the body. Also we may consider the relation of priestly wisdom to the wisdom of king and prophet.

III

'A fully developed culture', Christopher Dawson has written, 'involves a spiritual organization' which includes some 'type of spiritual élite', a class which 'forms and is formed by the sacred tradition which binds the whole culture together'. Though the character of this élite varies in different cultures, 'we find the same social types recurring to such an extent that it is possible to reduce their multiplicity to a few primary archetypes: those of Priest, King or Law-giver, Prophet or Seer'.[1]

The archetype we study here, that of wisdom embodied in a human figure, may appear in any of the three types named by Dawson. We have spoken of Jesus and of Gautama as the greatest prophets of whom we have record; and at this point it may be well to consider briefly the three types in their relation before choosing for closer study certain figures as types of priestly and of kingly wisdom within a particular situation.

We may again accept as starting point the description of the three types offered by Christopher Dawson in his study of the relations of religion and culture. Of the prophetic type he writes: it brings us 'beneath the surface of cultural tradition and social custom to the deepest levels of religious consciousness'; its function is to be to the community 'the mouthpiece of the divine will'. In exercise of this function the prophet may readily come into conflict with the priest, the guardian of established religious tradition. The priest Dawson describes as 'the man who is trained and set apart to perform the rites and ceremonies—above all the sacrifices —which form the essential bond between the society and its gods'. The king, or law-giver, 'is regarded as the personal representative or embodiment of divine power'.

This description of the king applies more obviously within the earlier form of culture, in which divine, and earthly or human, power and wisdom are hardly differentiated. As we try to follow the relation of type-figures of prophet, priest and king within later societies, we find the king embodying human, or secular, power over against the religious authority claimed by priest and prophet. From the history of our own

---

[1] *Religion and Culture* (Sheed & Ward, 1948), pp. 65-6.

country in the medieval period we may take the figures of
King Henry II and Archbishop Thomas Becket, in their
conflict, as an instance of the power over men's minds of
priestly wisdom in heroic stand against the force and wisdom
of a king. But first we may look back to the conflict in
earlier times of prophetic with priestly wisdom.

The teaching both of Gautama Buddha and of Jesus
Christ stood out against an older priestly tradition. That
tradition of ritual, and above all of sacrifice, which Gautama
sought to simplify—rejecting all but its moral and spiritual
significance—was already in his time of great antiquity. It
is, indeed, the most ancient priestly tradition of which any
full record survives. Scholars have traced its development,
through the second and first millenniums B.C., from a technique apparently aiming at material benefits only—wealth,
long life, victory—to a theory of mystic communion with an
eternal and all-embracing spiritual reality. The discovery
by Brahmin thinkers of identity between the self and
Brahman, the ultimate reality, was 'a revolutionary event
in the history of Indian religion', since recognition of the
supreme importance of this intuition 'rendered superfluous
the immense structure of ritual science and ceremonial
observance which had accumulated round the sacrifice'.[1]

Against this structure of sacrificial ritual, too deeply en-
trenched in the culture to be easily displaced, the Buddha
contended, rejecting it from the ethical rather than from the
metaphysical standpoint. 'Offering sacrifices' is included
among the 'low arts' from which Gautama 'holds aloof'.[2]
In the Kutadanta Sutta approval is given to an imagined
sacrifice in which no living thing is injured—the contrary of
the typical Vedic sacrifice. 'With ghee and oil and butter
and milk and honey only was that sacrifice accomplished'
yet even this pure offering is placed low as compared with
sacrifice that is moral and spiritual. Best of all is such

[1] *Religion and Culture*, p. 96.   [2] *Dialogues of the Buddha*, Part I, p. 26.

abstinence from evil, from lust and delusion, as characterizes the true recluse.

In the history of the Jewish people we find similarly a struggle against reliance upon the external form of sacrifice, and against the priestly class whose traditional wisdom included a technique of ritual observance. 'I will have mercy and not sacrifice': in this Word of the Lord the teaching of the earlier prophets culminates, and to this Word wide interpretation has been given in the teaching of Jesus. *Go ye and learn what this meaneth: 'I will have mercy and not sacrifice.'* These words were spoken when Pharisees had blamed Jesus for eating with publicans and sinners; and again, the Pharisees who blamed the disciples for plucking corn to eat on the Sabbath day are referred to the same saying: if they had known its meaning they 'would not have condemned the guiltless'. Thus, the contention of the prophets is understood as against the whole ritual attitude, its reliance on external form and precept rather than on love and insight.

For the people of India the teaching of the Buddha proved too austere. The missionary efforts of Asoka, Rhys Davids observes, causing the adherence of great numbers of nominal converts even hastened the faith's decline. In those lands where it persisted Buddhism was overgrown by beliefs and practices the Buddha would have condemned. Christianity also, when it became a state religion and was imposed by force or by prestige on converts little prepared for it, lost much of its spiritual character. In the eleventh century when Pope Gregory withstood Henry IV in the name of the Christian Church, and when, in the following century, Becket withstood Henry II, the Christian Church was the repository of a priestly tradition in which the sacrificial ritual of the Mass held a place as essential as ritual sacrifice had done in the priestly tradition of India and of Palestine.

Can we justly regard the conflict between Thomas Becket and Henry as a type instance of priestly against kingly wisdom? King Henry of England was not one of those great figures that stand as types of wisdom in the world's memory. Archbishop Becket was indeed a memorable figure; he has a place among our English 'folk heroes', a hero in courage and strength of purpose, in the esteem of many a saint and martyr, yet in his pride and rashness hardly a type of wisdom.

My choice here of his image, as it appears in historic record and poetic drama, is partly on account of the full documentation and literary treatment of his life and death, which allows us to examine the relation of the image to the minds that have cherished it as we cannot do in the case of a sage whose image has a lesser place in our literature. Then again, it is not so much Becket the man, but the priest, Thomas, Archbishop, that we consider. We have to look back, from the man embodying the priestly tradition at a particular place and time, to the events that had moulded that tradition and gathered the reverence that clung to the Archbishop in his offlce.

In Becket's life, as recorded for us, there is a point of transition when he assumes—it seems with reluctance—the full burden of that tradition. A conversation has been recorded between Becket and the Cardinal, Henry of Pisa, in which Becket spoke of his fears that the king was about to attack the rights of the Church in a manner which he, if made Archbishop, must resist at all costs. 'I shall earn the king's enmity and lose the friendship that has been the best thing in my life.' 'That', the Cardinal is said to have answered, 'is the sacrifice demanded of you.' 'But, above all, I am not worthy! I have lived in the world. I have fought in the army of the King. Who am I that I should lead the hosts of the Lord?' 'In serving the Church, my son, you will save your own soul.'[1]

[1] The words are so quoted in the study of Becket, in *Seven Archbishops*, by Sidney Dark, who presumably used the great volumes of *Materials for the History of Thomas Becket*.

The tradition of wisdom and moral authority pertaining to the Church which made the office of archbishop so great a responsibility in the view of Becket, and in his life a transforming power, had taken its distinctive form during the past eleven centuries of the Christian era. The fall of the Roman Empire, after Christianity had become a state religion, left to the dignitaries of the Church the duty of transmitting to the Empire's barbarian conquerors the tradition of culture and of government derived from Imperial Rome. '*Catholica fides*', Dr. Delisle Burns wrote in his study of medieval Christendom, 'had taken the place of that *fides Romana* which had been the moral basis of the Roman Empire. That Catholic faith, or loyalty, was a principle of moral cohesion within the wider society which embraced the turbulent growing societies of the nations under their different kings.' 'The most fundamental contribution to the progress of civilized life made by European Christendom was . . . its establishment of a community of feeling and experience among all men, women and children in Western Europe through sacraments, fasts and feasts and other religious customs. Medieval Europe was divided by a caste system in every locality and by the rivalry of independent lordships; but across these barriers *Catholica fides* united the serf with his Lord and the whole community in any one district with those of all others in the Latin Church which claimed to be universal.'[1]

Beside the hold upon men's emotions given to the Church through this widespread ritual observance, there was, concentrated in the bishop's office, an authority derived from the tradition both literary and administrative of Imperial Rome. As in the most ancient civilizations there was concentrated in the priesthood that *mana*, or magic power, which the written word and formulated law has for primitive minds, so in the early middle ages in Europe, power

[1] *The First Europe* (Allen & Unwin, 1947), p. 40.

over the warrior leader and his men pertained to the
priesthood that wrote and read the Latin language and
guarded the treasure of Roman legislation and learning.
Dr. Burns has included in his study of the moral authority
possessed by the Church of the First Europe some discussion
of the relation which the bishops of that time felt between
themselves and the prophet-priests of the Old Testament
stories. That divine authority by which Samuel could first
consecrate Saul, and then take from him the kingship to
confer it upon David, the bishops—and above all the Pope—
felt themselves to possess when they anointed with the
sacred oil the warrior king or deposed him through the
ritual of excommunication.

It is, I think, only through reflection on the power of this
tradition, investing with authority the dignitaries of the
Church, that we can at all understand the attitude of such
a priest as Becket in his struggle with the king. When we
read in the correspondence that passed between Archbishop
Thomas and his friend, John of Salisbury, their estimate of
the actual occupant of the Papal chair—'Rome was never
yet proof against bribes.' Even 'our Lord the Pope' is
sometimes driven to acts that 'may benefit the state but
cannot benefit religion'[1]—we are tempted to wonder how
this Rome and this pontiff can continue for John and for
Thomas to represent the Power to which they give allegiance,
and for which Thomas is glad to die. Such loyalty seems a
measure of the power of the archetypal image, the image of
divine wisdom and might, that for minds at particular
periods is so embodied in an office or institution that no
incongruity can dissociate it.

When we consider Archbishop Thomas himself as an
embodiment of the image in the minds of simple people
during, and still more after, his lifetime, we must recognize
the fusion with this of that other image, yet more mysterious,

[1] Quoted in *Thomas Becket* by Robert Speaight (Longmans, 1938), p. 167.

of atoning sacrifice. When on his ride from Sandwich to
Canterbury, 'multitudes of the poor' attended their returning archbishop, throwing their garments in his way and
crying, 'Blessed is he who cometh in the name of the Lord,'
the people's adoration one assumes to have been given to
the wisdom and goodness of their father in God; but the
faith that could work miracles, centred on St. Thomas after
his death, was given to the saint who by his sacrifice of life
for his Church had become more nearly one with the divine
Redeemer, able to heal and save through the merit of a
martyr's death.[1]

In an interesting comparison of passages from different
writers, contemporary and later, describing the Archbishop's murder, Dr. Edwin Abbott has shown something
of the influence, on the narratives, of the image of the
sacrificial death of Christ. The martyr's reported words are
modified to conform to those uttered by Jesus, and his
position at death is changed from 'under a column', and
turned 'to the northern part of the Church', to one immediately before the altar.[2]

The death of Becket that had already in the immediately
succeeding centuries become hallowed in men's minds has
again been so presented in *Murder in the Cathedral* by T. S.
Eliot. We may distinguish in the play different planes of
meaning, and may, I think, characterize them by reference
to a distinction made by Gabriel Marcel in the meaning of
the terms, 'problem' and 'mystery'.[3]

The problem Marcel defines through relation to the

[1] I do not find convincing the arguments of those who hold that Becket's
death was a ritual murder, so regarded both by himself and by the common
people. It may well be, however, that at the time images and practices of
the pagan religion, not yet, as later they were, officially discriminated and
condemned, were actively present in the minds of many; so that the drops
they cherished of the martyr's blood gained potency not only through
Christian teaching but also from conscious association with yet older rites
in which a kingly victim, or his substitute, died for his people.
[2] In *Saint Thomas of Canterbury: his Death and Miracles* (Black, 1898).
[3] In his essay 'On the Ontological Mystery' in *The Philosophy of Existence*
(Harvil Press, 1948).

attitude of the scientist, or scientific historian, who explains an event by analyzing its causes or conditions, while himself standing apart from it as a neutral observer. Human fear or desire may help to determine the scope of the problem, even the nature of its solution, yet no personal decision or response is felt to be involved. When we recognize mystery such neutrality, Marcel says, is not possible. We are forced to participate, to respond as to a presence.

In Eliot's play there are passages that invite us to recur to the historic or psychological problems offered by the conflict. We may ask which of the conflicting views was more for the world's advantage, or what were the motive forces, the conscious or subconscious impulses, involved. In other passages more inevitably, though indeed suffusing the whole play, mystery—in Marcel's sense of the word—confronts us. The action as communicated demands of us something of that participation expressed by the chorus through their proclaimed function as witnesses. 'We are forced to bear witness', the chorus chant at the opening of the play. The 'poor women of Canterbury', have come, forced by some 'presage of an act which our eyes are compelled to witness'; and to them as the hour approaches of his martyrdom the Archbishop declares the meaning of their witness:

> These things had to come to you and you to accept them.
> This is your share of the eternal burden,
> The perpetual glory.

The meaning these words convey is, I think, the same that Marcel has in mind in his discussion of the witness borne, or testimony given, to a mystery. Testimony, he says, using the word in its fullest sense, 'is based on fidelity to a light, or to use another language, to a grace received':[1] a grace, not here, he tells us, intended in its strictly

---

[1] 'Testimony and Existentialism, *op. cit.* pp. 72 and 73.

theological sense; but a grace or gift, as demanding response—such response as accepts, in the words of Eliot's drama, a share of the burden and glory of the thing witnessed.

The distinction between presentation of a mystery, demanding complete response, and of a problem, requiring only a solution by the intellect in detachment, is illustrated in Eliot's play through the contrast—the curious jolt of transition—we feel when the four knights who have committed the murder step, as it were, out of their place in the drama, to address, in a kind of jocular present-day idiom, the present-day audience.

The play, as a tragic action, has lacked so far what tragedy seems to require; the presence on both sides, if not of some right, yet of a point of view, a case that could be argued. Becket's case has been presented as no matter for argument, but as a spirit's triumph over natural impulses towards surrender that are but temptations. We, with the chorus, have witnessed, amid horrifying images of human guilt and desolation, the mystery of the Divine presence to man; the spirit, summoned by the Divine wisdom, entering after torment of inward conflict upon the peace of obedience.

The mystery of the Divine presence might have taken other forms. Among those who in the conflict of Church and State gave loyal support to King Henry, some may have seen him as representing for them divine power and wisdom. We know that in the dawn of civilization, at the very beginning of man's religious life, kingship was so regarded. As the devout catholic of the middle ages, though recognizing the infirmities of Our Lord, the Pope, yet continued in his allegiance, so from Ancient Egypt comes down to us the confession of faith of the scribe, who, troubled, yet remained assured that 'authoritative utterance', 'understanding', 'truth', were with his Divine king, even while he saw, through conformity to the royal commands, confusion and violence spreading through the land.[1]

In no such spirit of tragic loyalty do the knights in Eliot's play defend their action. Their arguments remain upon the problem level, cleverly recalling us, the present-day audience, to our commonsense view concerning the 'just subordination of the pretensions of the Church to the welfare of the State', suggesting that their act should be recognized as 'a first step' towards a state of things that has now gained approval. It is a plea the historian could hardly accept, but even a better argument in the context of the play would be swept aside. Argument is so dismissed by the Third Priest as, near the close of the play, he gives God thanks for another saint conjoined with all saints and martyrs, refusing to think further of the wretches weaving to justify themselves a fiction that ever unravels, 'pacing for ever in the hell of make believe'. Whatever may be our practical judgement concerning problems of Church and State, when, as in this play, we are made to feel that mystery has appeared, embodiment has been found of the archetype of the Divine wisdom, argument is silent, the problem attitude suspended.

Yet argument must be renewed. On the way to faith it has its place. For us perhaps neither prophet, priest, nor king, in their ancient form, stand clearly as representatives of the wisdom of God. Only in our own fashion, amidst our own bewildering problems of sense and intellect, can we glimpse upon the bestial floor, 'the uncontrollable mystery'.

IV

'A fully developed culture involves a spiritual organization.' These words of Christopher Dawson, already quoted,

[1] See *Kingship and the Gods*, by Henri Frankfort (University of Chicago Press and Cambridge University Press, 1948), p. 51.

suggest a question in regard to present-day society: does our present-day culture, lacking, it seems, distinctive religious belief, include nevertheless a spiritual organization within which individuals fulfil functions corresponding to those of the ancient prophet, priest, and king, thus in some degree embodying, as did these figures, different aspects of the archetype of wisdom?

Let us think first of kingship and kingly wisdom, not as it appeared in that strife between Church and State illustrated in the struggle between Becket and King Henry; but in its earliest form as studied in the records of ancient Egypt and Babylon.

In medieval Europe secular power and spiritual authority had fallen apart. In ancient Egypt, at least in some periods, the king represented the community in its completeness. Its secular powers of material force and directive human wisdom were embodied in him, and in addition he exercised the priestly function of mediating between the community and its gods.

We have referred already to that confession of faith in kingship made by the scribe who, in time of trouble and perplexity, wrote, addressing the king: 'Authoritative utterance [*hu*] is in thy mouth. Understanding [*sia*] is in thy heart. Thy speech is the shrine of truth [*maat*].' 'The king,' Henri Frankfort tells us, 'in the solitariness of his divinity, shoulders an immense responsibility', that of maintaining *maat*, 'which is usually translated "truth", but which really means "right order"—the inherent structure of creation of which justice is an integral part'.[1]

Concerning this most comprehensive notion of 'right order', Frankfort quotes a passage from another ancient text in which the dead King, Amenemhet I, is represented as saying: 'I was one who produced barley and loved the corn-god. The Nile respected me at every defile. None

[1] *Kingship and the Gods*, p. 51.

hungered in my years, nor thirsted in them. Men dwelt (in peace) through that which I wrought'. 'The king "produced barley" not merely in an indirect way, for instance by caring for the farmers or furthering agriculture, but through his own actions—by maintaining *maat*, the right order which allowed nature to function unimpaired for the benefit of man.'[1] Here, associated with kingship, is that notion of an order at once cosmic and moral, which appears under different names in different ancient civilizations; 'as *Rita* in India, *Asha* in Persia, the Greek *Dike* and *Moira*, and the Chinese *Tao*'.[2] The Egyptian king, as representing the great co-operative order of the agricultural society, could serve also as a mediating representative of those cosmic forces of nature with which the community had learnt to co-operate. That 'supernatural quality', inspiring wonder and terror, which belongs, Dawson has observed, to the leader or chief in the most primitive communities prior to the development of agriculture, would be felt with greater intensity in the king whose representative function endows him with the wonder of the new communal achievement of successful co-operation with hitherto alien and incalculable forces.[3]

If, with this archetypal pattern of kingship in mind, we think forward through the course of history to our own day, we find a breaking up of the characters present in ancient kingship. The function of political leadership, the control of the material force of the community, the exercise of moral or spiritual authority, become separable, both actually and in man's thought.

In our own time the supernatural quality pertaining to the 'gift of leadership', or to kingly wisdom, is felt but rarely. We shall speak presently of instances where the endowment of an elected individual, in relation to the great issues of the hour, called forth response as to the numinous. To the

[1] *op. cit.* p. 57.　　[2] *Religion and Culture*, p. 146.　　[3] *ibid.* pp. 110, 115.

office of king, apart from individual endowment, some traces
of supernatural quality seem still to adhere, enhancing for
us the value of the surviving institution as an emotionally
unifying force. But of the power over men's spirits of ancient
kingship we can have but glimpses. The image communicated through poetry can perhaps best help us to recover
imaginatively something of its hold upon emotion.

'A god is not so glorious as a king', muses one of Marlowe's
heroes, dreaming of the wearing of a crown 'whose virtue
carries with it life and death'. The words recall the ancient
pyramid text where the crown is invoked as a 'great
magician', and the newly succeeding king prays: Let there
be terror of me like the terror of thee. Let there be awe of
me like the awe of thee; love of me like the love of thee. If
we find in ourselves any response to such an invocation, or
to Marlowe's lines, we can perhaps recognize in that
response not only a relation to what anthropologists have
taught us was felt in old times, but also a revival of memories
from childhood. Kingship, as it was presented to our infancy
in fairy tales, interpreted through our feeling of magic
powers in our parents,[1] can fuse its influence with what our
adult minds imaginatively construct concerning kingship in
earlier periods of man's history.

But the archetype of kingship has a character more
profound than this childish wonder at magic power—a
character which can, I think, be felt in passages of Shakespeare's plays. In the tragedy of King-Lear, for instance,
the poetry of the great scene in which the broken king calls
on the elements, as on kindred powers, to avenge his wrongs,
makes us feel—overshadowing in terrible contrast the weakness and folly of the individual man—the mysterious, the

[1] With the revived infantile feeling of numinous power in the mother there
may fuse an image yet more ancient, that of the matriarch, the tribal
mother in times before kingship was known. This image is probably
influential when—as often in poetry—wisdom is represented in feminine
form. I have discussed this in *Archetypal Patterns in Poetry*,(Oxford University
Press, 1934), Ch. IV.

almost cosmic, majesty of kingship. It is this great image aroused in the mind of the spectator that can cause us to share the feeling of the attendant 'gentleman' for whom the pranks of Lear's madness are 'a sight most pitiful in the meanest wretch, Past speaking in a king.'

The ancient image of kingship was not of supernatural power only, but of wisdom as a divine gift beyond ordinary human capacity. Such divinely granted wisdom was possessed by the city kings whom Hesiod pictured guiding their small communities in the way of peace and order. The Hebrew records have provided an image more familiar, of the ideally wise king, in the story of the youthful Solomon, feeling the greatness of his charge and praying for an understanding heart to 'discern between good and bad; for who is able to judge this thy so great people?' And because the speech pleased the Lord, Solomon received the gift of understanding, together with riches and honour, so that there came of all people to hear him, and men said the wisdom of God was in him to do judgement. (I Kings, Chs. III and IV.)

Both these images show us wisdom assuaging internal conflicts; but part of the kingly function is to maintain the security of his people when their order and peace is threatened from without. In the ideal images of early kingship there could be little thought of persuasive wisdom, wise compromise, in relation to other communities. The ideal king secured the peace of his people by successful war, imposing order at the sword's point.

An image of kingly wisdom in war, and victory with an aura of divinity about it, has been fashioned by a poet of our own time, upon the legendary victory, over heathen hordes, of the British king Arthur at Mount Badon.

The words that have come down to us describing this victory tell of an onslaught by Arthur when there fell nine hundred and sixty men, 'and none slew them but he

alone'.[1] The words recall those expressions in art which
Frankfort adduces as characteristic of the image of kingship
in ancient Egypt, where a victory is represented by 'the
single symbolical figure of the ruler', sometimes slaying
'a plurality' of the enemy, or holding a mass of helpless
captives. If we 'probe the full meaning' of the scene depicted,
we see, Frankfort asserts, that 'the enemies in the design
represent an element of chaos. . . . Victory is not mere
assertion of power; it is the reduction of chaos to order.'[2]

'Reduction of chaos to order': these words describe also
the image which Charles Williams' poem fashions of the
victory of Mount Badon as experienced by his poet-hero
Taliessin.[3]

Williams uses the suggestion of the late R. G. Collingwood
that an actual historical Arthur may have won his victory
through the wisdom of his reliance on 'a mobile field-army',
a force of cavalry of which the Saxon invaders had none,
'and very little tactical cohesion'.[4] The poem pictures
Taliessin, King Arthur's poet and 'captain of horse',
stationed upon a ridge, looking down upon the battle; his
force 'hidden behind, as the king's mind had bidden'. The
pirate-enemy, unlike the king's army, lacked support;
'neither for charge nor for ruse could the allied crews abide
the civilized single command'. As Taliessin sits waiting:

> Suddenly the noise abated, the fight vanished, the last
> few belated shouts died in a new quiet
> In the silence of a distance, clear to the king's poet's sight,
> Virgil was standing on a trellised path by the sea.
> Taliessin saw him negligently leaning; he felt
> the deep breath dragging the depth of all dimension,
> as the Roman sought for the word, sought for his thought,
> Sought for the invention of the City by the phrase.

[1] From the history by the monk Nennius, written in the ninth century A.D.
[2] *Kingship and the Gods*, pp. 7, 8 and 9.
[3] 'Mount Badon' in *Taliessin through Logres* (Oxford University Press, 1938).
[4] *Arthurian Torso* by C. S. Lewis (Oxford University Press, 1948), p. 9.

We are told[1] that 'the city' stood to Williams for an idea
that always haunted him, that London, the actual city that
he loved, was to him 'an image—an imperfect, pathetic,
heroic and majestic image—of Order'. Virgil, 'the poet *par
excellence* of "the city" ', seeking his thought and 'the word',
is not only celebrating the greatness of Rome, teaching
men to reverence their city more truly; he is about to
impose order, by a great line of verse, upon the chaos of
thought and language, as Taliessin, in obedience to
'the king's mind', through his charge at the right point
and right moment, will impose order on the confusion
of the battle.

Then, in the moment of the victorious charge, when the
force and violence of the heathen onset, 'the thudding
hammer of Thor', is mastered by 'the grand art'—that is in
Taliessin's vision the art both of planned warfare and of
poetry—another overtone of meaning enters. The image of
the Christ appears, seen as in the Apocalypse, 'snowy-haired,
brazen-footed'. The household of Taliessin, as they swung
into the battle, flash in his eyes as 'hierarchs of freedom,
golden candles of the solstice that flared round the golden-
girdled Logos'.

The poem has beauty, and power through the cumulative
weight of association with which it charges this battle
image. The rendering is true to the ancient tale of
Arthur's victory, bringing a time of peace and order to a
Britain shattered by barbarian raids—a time of peace so
blessed in memory that in the countryside men long
cherished the prophesy of an undying Arthur destined to
return. The use of the apocalyptic image shedding glory
on the battle is true to an older, more universal memory
and emotion.

Written before 1938, this poem belonged to a world that
had not yet experienced the last terrors war has revealed.

[1] In *Arthurian Torso*, p. 105.

With these present to us, and the threat shadowing us of another war that might complete civilization's destruction, there is something terrifying in the glory that poetry can shed on war and the wisdom of war, through appeal to deeply inherited racial experience.

A theory of human evolution has been recently elaborated which asserts that man's mentality has been biased to make him the willing subject of 'a dual code' of morality. The evolutionary fashioning of man's mind was accomplished, Sir Arthur Keith believes, within local groups whose members practised a dual code, of sympathy and co-operation within the group, of suspicion, hostility, contempt, toward those beyond its borders. By the duality of feeling thus established through the ages of human history, Keith explains the extreme difficulty which prophet-teachers have experienced in turning men's hearts towards a code of universal compassion and good-will.[1]

In some respects this theory seems open to question, but there is surely no error in its emphasis upon the duality of man's emotional nature, and in its corollary concerning human resistance to the teaching of love. Jesus taught the brotherhood of man and the love of enemies. Yet quickly this teaching was transformed in conformity with the code of nature: thou shalt love thy friend and hate thine enemy. When my enemy is the enemy of my group and can thus be deemed the enemy of God, hatred can be magnified by religion. The terrible image from the Apocalypse that, in the poem cited, sheds a glory of divinity on the battle, may recall to our thought how the image of Christ in historic transformation became a warrior figure, one in whose name men could ride 'to their horses' bridles' in the blood of the heathen. The feeling and assumptions of the priest who could use these words, and could speak of the slaughter thus rhetorically magnified as the 'marvellous judgement of

---

[1] *A New Theory of Human Evolution*, by Arthur Keith (London, 1948).

God'[1] seem not out of accord with the feeling of the seer in whose vision Christ, the Logos, rode before his armies to 'make war upon the nations, to smite them with the sword proceeding from his mouth and to rule them with a rod of iron'. (Rev. XIX, 13.) In the seer of Patmos, in the medieval crusader, and in every poet singing the glory of war imposing right order, one feels the influence of the fatally dual morality the evolutionary process has taught mankind.

'Fatal' is the word that comes to one's lips to-day for the duality that makes men, who within their own community are co-operative and kindly, suspicious and hostile towards those of alien outlook, indifferent to cruelty inflicted upon them. In the course of man's earliest history the 'dual code' may have been, as Arthur Keith suggests, a means of developing in local groups valuable human qualities. In later ages there may have been no discoverable way of securing a precarious order among men than the way of war—human valour directed by a leader whose wise strategy could make the right response to the challenge of his time. But in our day is it any longer true that kingly wisdom can meet by way of war the time's challenge? Man's power over the elements has changed, it seems, the character of the challenge that the leaders of great states must meet. So terrible have become the effects of world war, upon the nominal victor as well as upon the vanquished, that for a great people the wisdom that is to find the way of salvation must follow the knife-edge path between destruction through war and submission to tyranny. Both wisdom in the leader, and response in the people to be led in this way of peace,

---

[1] The exultant words describing torture and slaughter of the Saracens, and telling how 'in the temple and porch of Solomon one rode in blood up to the knees and even to the horses' bridles, by the just and marvellous judgement of God', were spoken by Raymond of Agiles, 'one of the clergy in the train of Count Raymond of Toulouse and an eye witness of the capture of Jerusalem in the first crusade'. (Quoted in *The Mediaeval Mind*, by H. O. Taylor.)

are far harder to achieve than wisdom and response in the way of war, since in our heritage there is such opposition to peace, and to the temper of mind and spirit through which peace might be achieved. We may illustrate this from our own recent history.

Two brief periods there were—moments, we may say, in history—when the embodied archetype of kingly leadership seemed to shine like a star before multitudes.

In that moment in the last great war when Britain's fortunes were darkest, Winston Churchill rallied the courage of his fellow countrymen, having behind him a record of foresight and unwearied effort to secure response to the danger he foresaw, having also in full the muses' gift of persuasive, stirring eloquence. The people of Britain, and others beyond the seas, thrilled to his words and example of courage and steadfastness, and through the long struggle, the suffering and privations of the war, leadership and response did not fail. Behind them was the whole heritage, instinctive and traditional, of loyalty and comradeship within a group at war, and, toward the group's opponents, of antagonism to the death.

At the close of the other great war that fell within our century, there was a moment when for multitudes a figure seemed to embody the ideal of a messiah of peace. That ideal image we find in Hesiod—the king to whom the muses grant wisdom and eloquence, who with knowledge and sureness of speech can abate the mightiest contention— seemed fulfilled not within the limits of a single city but within a warring world. Many writers have testified to the hope and reverence with which President Woodrow Wilson was greeted by the people of Europe when he first came among them in 1918. 'He enjoyed', said Maynard Keynes, 'a prestige and a moral influence throughout the world unequalled in history.' Keynes speaks of his 'bold and measured words' that 'carried to the peoples of Europe

above and beyond their own politicians'. The enemy peoples
trusted him, 'the allied peoples acknowledged him not as a
victor only but almost as a prophet'.[1] Leonard Woolf has
written of the 'short period' when 'the world itself, the
millions of puzzled, disquieted, inarticulate persons who had
fought the war' looked to President Wilson to bring them a
peace 'based upon the lessons of the past'.[2] He came to
suffering Europe, it seemed, as Hesiod's wise kings came
among their fellow-citizens, to give 'binding decisions, clear
and just'.

'The disillusion was so complete', wrote Keynes, 'that
some of those who had trusted most hardly dared speak of
it.' Not the terms of the Versailles Treaty only, betrayed
men's hope, but, above all, the failure of President Wilson
to secure America's participation in the League of Nations—
the institution planned with so much faith and aspiration as
a means to world peace. On this failure we look for the
verdict of history. Was President Wilson, for all his good-
will—his passionate dedication of himself, even to the death,
to the way of peace as he conceived it—still betrayed not
only by his fellow-men but also by falsity within?

'Woodrow Wilson', says one writer—attempting a psychological study of the President's failure—'was incapable
of rising above his own self-sufficiency and his hatred of
political foes.' From this hate and this incapacity followed
the 'two miscalculations' which made failure inevitable.[3]
Concerning the miscalculations, and their effect, there seems
little doubt now. The President brought with him from
America to the Paris conference no member of the party
opposed to his own. Before leaving the States he had issued
an appeal to the country to support him at Paris—an appeal

---

[1] *The Economic Consequences of the Peace*, by J. M. Keynes (Macmillan, 1920),
pp. 34-5.
[2] *After the Deluge*, by L. Woolf (first published 1931, reissued in Pelican
Books, 1937), p. 55.
[3] *Men of Stress*, by Harley Williams (Cape, 1948), p. 144.

which even at the time was recognized, in the words of a letter written by President Eliot of Harvard, as an 'inexpedient departure' from his position previously maintained as 'President of the United States, claiming and having the support of the entire people'. The failure of the President to survey and rise above party conflict, as he could survey conflict in Europe, was summed up in a characterization of his attitude by Churchill: 'Peace and goodwill among all nations abroad, but no truck with the Republican party at home.'[1] The effect of this surrender to party spirit was seen in the Republican hostility that led to the refusal of the Senate to ratify the Treaty and Covenant of the League. To the President's failure, both here and at the Paris Conference, to achieve his aims also contributed that 'self sufficiency' or spiritual isolation, that debarred him from co-operating freely with those of his own party who could have helped him through possession of gifts different from his own. As with the leader so also was it with those whose hopes he had represented. Throughout the struggle for a wise treaty and an effective League, always in the background was the inability of the peoples to rise above their national and group hatreds and impulses of vengeance.

Whether in the dangers threatening us to-day, of further disastrous world war, any leader, or fortunate succession and co-operation of leaders, will appear having wisdom to find a way of freedom and peace, and will win response from the peoples, and our civilization be saved, the future will reveal. The lesson of the past is clear concerning the danger of that same self- and group-centred intolerance blinding men to wisdom, that once in the history of Christendom transformed the Christ, the teacher of love, into the warrior-god leading his crusaders to the torture and slaughter of the heretic and the heathen.

[1] Quoted by Harley Williams, *loc. cit.*

From the thought of kingly wisdom—wise leadership in things temporal—we may turn to that other aspect of wisdom we term 'spiritual', concerned with eternal values, an aspect represented in the past by the figures of prophet and priest. The question was raised whether in our present-day culture—unlike that of the middle ages as dominated by science rather than by religious belief—a function is still fulfilled by individuals, outside as well as within the churches, corresponding to that in former times exercised by the Christian priesthood.

By those who believe there are sacramental mysteries mediating between God and man of which the Christian Church is the unique guardian, this question can be summarily answered in the negative. Similarly those who believed in 'the Divine right of kings' would have been outraged by the assumption made in our discussion of kingly wisdom and leadership, that this could belong to individuals not consecrated within the ancient institution of kingship. Those of us who believe that neither consecrated king nor priest becomes uniquely a channel of divine grace are free to answer, or attempt to answer, questions concerning the function and influence of individuals according to what seems the evidence of social experience.

In the dark ages of Europe, after the fall of the Roman Empire, one function of the Christian priesthood was in relation to kingship. To the barbaric warriors they consecrated as kings the bishops gave moral authority over their subjects; also they brought to these kings a tradition of administrative wisdom derived from imperial Rome; and could sometimes by threat and exhortation curb the cruelty of kingly rule. We may ask is a similar function exercised by any class of men to-day? Is a similar service of support, counsel, criticism, offered to those who in key positions of power bear the responsibility of that kingly leadership by which our civilization may be saved or wrecked?

The other, yet more distinctive, duty of the Christian priesthood was to maintain, in those who laboured and suffered under kingly rule, a vision of spiritual fulfilment within and beyond their temporal sufferings. It has always been the faith of priest and prophet that if material civilization must perish, the earthly city fall, there remains a heavenly city; the divine meaning and purpose glimpsed within this sphere of space and time must be fulfilled, if not here, in some other dimension of being. Is this faith still maintained among us, ministered in some fashion to those outside, as well as within, the influence of the churches?

An answer, or the frame of an answer, to our question has been suggested in the notable book by Julien Benda, *La Trahison des Clercs*.[1] The title in itself offers a phrase expressive of a thought present in the minds of many concerned about the life of our time. By taking over from the history of the Church in Europe the term 'clerk' as denoting all who, in distinction from the unlettered mass, had direct access to tradition sacred and secular; applying this term to all those whose distinctive occupation in any age is with tradition—the religious, literary, or scientific heritage—suggesting also that such privileged access is a responsibility that can be betrayed, Benda has outlined a definite theme which seems worthy of consideration in the light of conditions and ideas that have changed since 1927 when his book was written.

Though Benda, defining broadly the term 'clerk', includes under it all 'who seek their joy in the practice of an art or a science or metaphysical speculation', in his comparison of clerks past and present he regards chiefly writers on general themes, moral, philosophic—men of wide-ranging thought and influence such as Aquinas, Leonardo da Vinci, Erasmus,

[1] Translated by Richard Aldington as *The Great Betrayal* (Routledge, 1923).

Goethe, Voltaire. The theme of our present discussion being the image of wisdom as operative in the past and present, we shall follow Benda in thinking of the clerks—those who, it is suggested, correspond to the old-time sages, priests and prophets—as men of wide-ranging thought and insight, not scientific specialists; since wisdom has always been held to include more than learning or knowledge. The 'clerks', we may say, are those who maintain, with fresh application, correction, enlargement, a tradition concerned with man's whole nature, imaginative, emotional, spiritual, as well as intellectual, sensuous.

In regarding such thinkers as fulfilling a need corresponding to that met by a priesthood in societies organized on a religious basis, we may strengthen our argument by looking back at such societies as were not penetrated by belief in any uniquely divine revelation.

Such a society was that of China as moulded by the teaching of Confucius, a teaching carried on to later ages by 'Confucian scholars', whom Dawson includes with the priesthood of other societies, under the title of 'a spiritual élite'. Confucius and the scholars who followed him made no claim to a divine revelation, yet they possessed a religious philosophy in their conception of a sacred moral order governing the life of society as well as the life of nature, an order handed down by ancestral tradition. Confucius, Dawson argues, is rightly regarded as the founder of a religion in that he taught the necessity of a new relation of inward conformity to the ancient external order of ritual and law. The sacred rites he continued to venerate would, Confucius held, lack efficacy unless those who honoured them practised also the virtues of sincerity and loyalty in human relationships.[1]

The culture of the ancient Greeks, above all of Athens in the time of that city's greatness, affords another instance,

[1] *Religion and Culture*, p. 164.

more familiar to our thought and feeling, of an élite possessing spiritual wisdom without claim to divine revelation.
For us the poetry of Aeschylus, the philosophy of Plato,
present a wisdom that is part of life to-day. Aeschylus
offered as poetry, not as dogma, the great myths he
fashioned, of Prometheus, of the Eumenides, that still represent truly for us aspects of human suffering and achievement.
Plato, also presenting vivid myths—of man's imprisonment
in the flesh, of his eternal kinship and destiny—has warned
his hearers how such myths are to be accepted. Though
there is lure and enchantment in them, there is also hazard.[1]
Both the myth-maker and those who hear him, being but
men, should demand no more than 'a likely story' of things
beyond man's capacity (*Timaeus*). We who have an awareness more confirmed and continuous than had Plato of the
dangers that beset those who venture in thought beyond the
range of human experience, find that such occasional
warnings, with recognition of the value and limits of myth,
bring us nearer in sympathy to the Greek philosopher and
poet than we can be to those who would impose as authoritative any traditional belief that human experience cannot
verify.

Let us return to the comparison Benda has invited us to
make between thinkers of our day and representative
'clerks' of the past, such as Erasmus, Kant, Goethe. These
and other such sages, though they could not change the
greed and violence of worldly men, could and did uphold
an ideal of wisdom that shamed such passions. Only the
'clerks' in his own day, Benda complains, 'have adopted
political passions'; a 'majority of men of letters, and many
scholars, philosophers and "ministers" of the divine, share
in the chorus of hatreds among races and political factions.'[2]
Between the date of Benda's book and the present, there

---

[1] *Phaedrus*, 114.　　　　　　　　[2] *op. cit.* p. 31.

has been change, I think, in the general attitude of those we may term 'clerks'; but the point I wish now to consider is the manner in which Benda conceives the responsibility of the clerks towards political movements and their leaders. All through his discussion he distinguishes sharply between political aims and methods, and those of the true clerk, concerned with abstract truth and justice. In censuring those present-day thinkers who have inflamed racial and political passions, he appears also to censure all participation in political activity. His great representative clerks either 'said with Goethe "Let us leave politics to the diplomats and soldiers" ' or 'gazing as moralists upon the conflict of human egotisms, like Erasmus, Kant, Renan, they preached, in the name of humanity or justice, the adoption of an abstract principle superior to and directly opposed to these passions'.[1]

At the present time it seems that we must recognize a different relation of the clerks to politics. In view of the urgent need in politics for disinterested thought and action, it has become clear that those having special opportunities for thought and study should not merely look on in detachment at the conflict of human egotisms. Since it is only in meeting the challenge of concrete situations that wisdom can be truly applied, the thinker must enter these situations, if not through active participation, yet through the completest possible understanding and imaginative sympathy. In making his wisdom relevant to temporal circumstance, he must accept the inevitable risk of error that judgement in a concrete situation involves.

This element of risk and commitment in judgements we are bound to make has been emphasized by those philosophers who are to-day termed 'existentialists'. In their view the same tragic responsibility is borne by the thinker as by the man of action. The philosophic thinker is himself an individual subject, asking questions to which there are no

[1] *oq. cit.* pp. 30, 32.

completely satisfactory answers, obliged by his own nature
to make choices and decisions which his reason cannot fully
justify. If he ventures 'in the name of humanity or justice'
to criticize some action of his country's leaders, he does so
not as one possessing a criterion of absolute justice, but as
one committed, after use of all available resources, to a
precarious judgement as to relative justice in a complex and
unique situation.

Let us take as an instance the criticism by Maynard
Keynes of the terms of the Versailles treaty, and of the
action of those who designed them. In the introductory
chapter of his *Economic Consequences of the Peace*, Keynes has
indicated the attitude in which, as a member of the Supreme
Economic Council of the Allied Powers, he witnessed the
making of the Treaty—'witnessed' in that complete sense
Gabriel Marcel has suggested the term should bear. During
the six months he had spent in Paris after the armistice,
Keynes had so far transcended the preoccupations of an
individual Englishman as to become, he tells us, 'a European
in his cares and outlook', aware of the inter-relations and
common tragic involvement of all the countries of Europe.
Through this awareness his participation as a witness in 'the
proceedings of Paris' became a sense of the mystery of man's
smallness and blindness 'before the great events confronting
him'.[1] His book, with its condemnation of the treaty and
criticism of its makers, was the work of one who, using
whatever special resources he possessed, must take finally the
risks of decision, and could not 'disinterest himself from the
further unfolding of the great historic drama'.

Of Maynard Keynes it has been said that he was both
specialized thinker and 'a man of affairs determined so to
express his ideas that they should have the maximum
practical influence on public policy'. He made it his life's
work to save capitalism by altering its nature. 'The structure

[1] *op. cit.* pp. 3-4.

of his own economic thinking was built on his assumption that it was possible to persuade the capitalist in his own interest to abandon *laissez-faire* in favour of planning for the public good.'[1] Such an assumption, emotionally prompted, may well be mistaken; but so may any other that men dare to make in projecting improvement in human affairs. Would such an attitude as that of Keynes come under Benda's censure as the adopting of political passions? Keynes, like other thinkers who have dared to make their thought relevant to action in a changing, inadequately known, reality, has been censured for wrong estimates, and for ill consequences of his writings that he could not foresee. Yet it can be rightly maintained, I think, that it is only by entering, as Keynes did, the political situation, applying there at whatever risk, the philosophic thinker's wider outlook and sympathies, that the 'clerk' can influence and help to redeem political action.

By many of the religious thinkers of our time this necessity has been realized. As an instance we may take a pronouncement by the Assembly of the World Council of Churches at Amsterdam in 1948.

The task of the Assembly has been described as, first, a clarifying by the Churches, in the light of their different traditions, of their own understanding of their faith, and secondly, a real application of that faith to the conflicts and problems of modern society.[2] In the Report of Commission III, presented to and accepted by the Assembly,[3] occurs this passage: 'The Christian Churches should reject the ideologies of both communism and *laissez-faire* capitalism, and should seek to draw men away from the false assumption that these extremes are the only alternatives. Each has made promises which it could not redeem. Communist

[1] Article by the Editor, *The New Statesman and Nation*, 27 April 1946.
[2] *The Christian News-Letter*, 4 September 1946, p. 5.
[3] Printed in the third Amsterdam Volume. *The Church and the Disorder of Society* (S.C.M. Press).

ideology puts the emphasis upon economic justice and
promises that freedom will come automatically after the
completion of the revolution. Capitalism puts the emphasis
upon freedom and promises that justice will follow as a
by-product of free enterprise; that too, is an ideology which
has been proved false. It is the responsibility of Christians
to seek new, creative solutions which never allow either
justice or freedom to destroy the other.'

In the Assembly the Russian Churches were not represented. The American Churches were both represented and
the largest financial contributors to the Council. The
passage quoted from the Report—in Great Britain readily
accepted—in the States roused indignation. Even a judgement couched in such general terms seemed to many in the
States a provocative statement taking sides with the British
rather than with the American political outlook. The
Christian Century, 'one of the largest religious journals in the
United States, accused the American representatives of
having been dragged into conformity with the leftist beliefs
of the Churchmen of Europe', and went on 'to accuse the
Report of transferring the Church's concern "from the
spiritual business of converting men to the secular business
of converting men's institutions" '.[1]

In relation to this effort of Churchmen to apply their
spiritual insight to the political situation, the terms of the
criticism called forth may focus for us the question: Can
there be any secular business which should engage men's
will and intelligence and not their spirit, their religious
insight also? At the time of that saying of Jesus, 'Render
unto Caesar . . .' that seemed to divide the spiritual from
the secular sphere—the things of God from the the things
of Caesar—Caesar's power was virtually unapproachable by
those to whom Jesus spoke. Against the power of Rome he

[1] This account of 'American reactions' is taken from *The Christian News-
Letter*, 16 March 1949.

knew his countrymen, attempting revolt, would break themselves in vain. Besides he had interpreted the prophets as
telling of a direct and immediate intervention of God to do
for men what they could not achieve for themselves. Now
that we conceive men as responsible for their own institutions, the work of transforming them to some pattern nearer
the Divine Will becomes our religious task, a challenge to
all those in any way fitted to undertake it.

A somewhat similar distinction, false for us to-day,
between spiritual and secular, vitiates, I believe those con-
clusions concerning our present-day culture which appear
in the work, already mentioned, by the sociologist, P. A.
Sorokin. Like those who think of religion as concerned with
heavenly things in distinction from affairs of earth, Sorokin
distinguishes sharply between the 'ideational' type of
culture, where attention is directed towards Reality conceived as spiritual, eternal, and the 'sensate' type concerned
with the material, the transient. That our present culture
is concerned directly with the transient world known to our
senses cannot be questioned. But the question can be raised
whether the knowledge and control of the transient at which
we so strenuously aim shuts us out from encounter with the
spiritual and eternal. To Sorokin it appears to do so. Of
man and his history, in our time an 'economic', and a
'physiological-sensual, interpretation' have been given, and
such interpretations, Sorokin asserts, have excluded any
realization of man as a being of absolute value, a participant
in the Divine.[1] Those who have attempted the scientific
study of man have conceived him as a mere organism
motivated by sex or by greed; and in accordance with this,
the imaginative writers of to-day, Sorokin rhetorically
declares, have descended 'from the heavenly heights'
and 'heroic plateaux' of the earlier Ideational and
Idealistic literature 'to the earthly Main Street' and to

[1] *Social and Cultural Dynamics*, Vol. I, p. 641; Vol. III, p. 539.

poverty-stricken, demoralized and mentally-stricken persons and their affairs.[1]

Sorokin's description of the writers and artists of our time is a statement, more comprehensive than that of Julien Benda, of the same view, that the 'clerks' of to-day have betrayed their responsibility to the community to keep alive in it awareness of the spiritual, the eternal. To the sweeping indictment one can oppose only the conviction of those who have felt such an awareness communicated by the philosophic and imaginative writings of our day: an awareness of Divine encounter, mediated through those material conditions of which these writers seek to convey conceptual truth or emotional realization. A few instances may be cited to illustrate this communication of the spiritual through the material; and these same instances may perhaps suggest something of the manner in which 'clerks' of to-day fulfil the function of embodying, or presenting newly for us, the archetype of wisdom that in different forms men have reverenced through the ages.

If among imaginative writings of our time we think first of poetry, and wish to choose a poem pre-eminent among those that have had wide influence in recent years, there comes to mind *The Waste Land* by T. S. Eliot. So much has been written in comment on this poem that no attempt need be made here to estimate its many-sided significance. The one aspect of the poem essential for our purpose is its manner of communicating spiritual reality in terms relevant to the distinctive thought and feeling of our time.

That the poem has this relevance seems clear from the extent and character of the response expressed by many readers. I choose as illustration a few sentences from a recent tribute to T. S. Eliot. 'For my generation', Kathleen

[1] *op. cit.* Vol. III, pp. 539, 648.

Raine has written,[1] 'T. S. Eliot's early poetry, more than the work of any other poet, has enabled us to know our world imaginatively. . . . Eliot has shown us . . . that the statement of a terrible truth has a kind of healing power. . . . In his statement of the worst Eliot has always implied the whole extent of the reality of which that worst is only part. . . . The shallow philosophies both religious and secular of our parents' generation sought to eliminate evil from the world. Mr. Eliot's vision of hell restored a necessary dimension to our universe.'

The early poetry, of which *The Waste Land* is the most complete example, tells of a 'worst' that implies a whole beyond it and in the telling brings 'a kind of healing'. If we characterize this communicated worst in Kathleen Raine's words as a 'vision of hell', we may glance at those references to Dante's *Inferno* that, occurring in the first and last sections of Eliot's poem, relate the contemporary to the medieval image of a 'necessary dimension' of the apprehended universe.

The first of these references links the crowd that in the *Unreal city, Under the brown fog of a winter dawn, flowed over London Bridge*, with the unfortunates seen by Dante in the first stage of his descent, the many, undone by death, who in life made no choice between good and evil, and who now sustain an aimless perpetual motion, shut out alike from Heaven and deep Hell. Of this hurrying crowd, in Dante's vision, the wailing resounds through the starless air; in the Waste Land the like crowd exhale only such sighs as for Dante express the sadness without torment of the souls who by destiny, not will, lacked the true faith.

The reference in the last section of Eliot's poem is to the low frozen Hell where Dante saw traitors for ever imprisoned within their earthly agony and mutual hatred.

[1] In *T. S. Eliot, A Symposium*, compiled by R. March and Tambimuttu (Poetry London, 1948), pp. 78-9.

Something of a like doom the poet of the Waste Land has seen overshadowing us who, *each in his prison* of individual isolation, *have heard the key Trun in the door.* Yet in the same moment is heard the thunder-voice that might break the prison. By that voice is given the implication of what lies beyond, as, in the earlier reference, the gloom of the unreal city in the dawn-fog is pierced by recall of the rebirth mystery, the corpse buried, the seed planted, in fear and hope.

A reflective reader may follow one after another of the many lines of association that in Eliot's poem lead from its concrete imagery into far realms of myth and history. Though the poem may certainly be enjoyed while many of its allusions remain obscure, yet it is, I think, when felt against a vast background, literary and historic, that the true power of the imagery appears. A critic has spoken of a poet's 'sense of his own age' as a quality highly valued by Eliot, and noted how this sense is no mere familiarity with superficial contemporary detail, but an honesty that penetrates through this to grasp 'the intrinsic elements of life', the same from one epoch to another. Thus, the imagery in *The Waste Land* of the sordid life in a great city, of sterile lust and boredom, is raised to tragic intensity when felt in relation to such realms of death and times of bafflement as myth-makers and poets have imaged from the dawn of human history. The pattern, or archetype of rebirth, present in all nature and human life, and giving both foundation and expression to the perennial springing of human hope, can only be felt in power when the range of suggestion possible to poetic speech enables us to survey our present ills, pictured in vivid actuality, and yet in widest perspectives of space and time. It is because *The Waste Land* pre-eminently achieves this synthesis of present and past, of the sensuous actuality of contemporary life with life's unchanging pattern as expressed in the great religious myths,[1] that it seems in itself a refutation of the view that makes sharp division between secular and religious, temporal and eternal.

It may be, however, to prose-fiction rather than to poetry that the sociologist naturally looks for confirmation of his diagnosis of contemporary culture. The novel, even when it rises to the level of art, lacks that element of incantation, opening wider ranges of the hearer's mind, that the rhythm of poetry brings to its suggested ideas and concrete pictures. The novel makes its appeal to a wider audience and reflects more nearly the everyday consciousness. If in the ranges of contemporary thought and feeling which the novel expresses, we find presented an image of wisdom showing a distinctive form of spiritual awareness, it seems likely that this form is organic to our present culture.

Such organic relation between spiritual awareness and contemporary culture has been denied by a writer whose outlook is, I think, more penetrating than that of Sorokin. Christopher Dawson is not merely concerned, as Sorokin seems to be, to make distinction between the spiritual and the secular in a form so far hardened and verbalized as to serve as basis for statistical inquiry. In his study of religions Dawson has felt more deeply the interpenetration within experience of different elements and functions. Yet his vision of what is essential in religion determines him to feel that these essentials are not realized by those minds in our present society for whom the catholic faith has become

---

[1] This character, in its effect on the reader, has been, I think, illumined by a metaphor used by Arthur Koestler in his book, *Insight and Outlook* (Macmillan, 1949,)p. 331. He speaks of art, and poetry in particular, as teaching us to 'earth' our 'personal predicament' or 'particular miseries'. As the tensions and vibrations of an electrically charged body find outlet when 'contact is established with the earth and its infinitely greater absorptive capacity', so the tension of our self-regarding, feeling-saturated thoughts is relieved when these thoughts are linked with, and pass into, thoughts of those archetypal relations that we recognize as 'rooted in the very essence of the human condition'. Koestler's analogy offers more general terms for the effect described by Kathleen Raine as a healing through restoration of 'a necessary dimension to our universe'.

impossible. The Christian religion, identified with the institution of the Church, survives, he recognizes, 'and in certain respects flourishes', but 'has lost the organic relation with culture' which it possessed in the middle ages. 'Thus we have a secularized scientific world culture which is a body without a soul; while on the other hand religion maintains its separate existence as a spirit without a body.'[1]

Is there then no form of spiritual awareness and striving, whether or not to be identified with Christianity, which is organically related to contemporary social life? To the present writer it seemed, on meeting that statement of faith by Martin Buber to which reference has already been made, that this faith was related as spirit to the body of our present culture; however incomplete, as always, has been the penetration by the spirit of its organism. Those 'clerks' of our day who have found a medium of expression through the novel, as well as those who have written in more abstract philosophic terms, have communicated, I would suggest, awareness of spirit in the manner that Buber asserts spirit must be realized, as between the *I* and *Thou*, through personal relationship; and this realization is not alien to the actual striving of our time. While, through both philosophic and imaginative writing, the contrast becomes clearer between the true and the false—the spiritual and the merely instinctive or daemonic[2]—in human relationships, in actual intercourse also, and in the social movements of our time, we recognize a corresponding effort. In the struggle to realize democracy in both economic and political life, to extend justice and fellowship to backward and exploited peoples, to achieve completer understanding between men and women, parents and children, and between other persons of inevitably differing outlook—in all these efforts so

[1] *Religion and Culture*, p. 216.
[2] 'Daemonic' when the instinct to possess sexually, or dominate, while extended and made subtle by human intellect, remains uncontrolled by human respect and fellowship.

characteristic of our time, so much part of a culture in the widest sense scientific, we can discern, I think, the operation of a spirit organic to our present culture, though at war with much in the present; the same spirit that becomes increasingly articulate through writers of to-day.

To illustrate this thesis at all adequately in small compass is difficult, or indeed impossible; so many and widely different are the ways in which different writers have indicated the ideal of personal relationship. We may, however, glance at a few instances where the presence can be felt of this ideal; and it need not surprise us if we find it indicated rather through implicit condemnation of its opposite than positively. Even so imaginative writers of the Middle Ages gave expression to their ideal of Christian virtue through depicting satirically the vices of the time.

In our age the way of life that most outrages our perception of the spiritual is that which in pursuit of wealth or power treats persons merely as means. As notable portraits of the man of business, or of property, whose distinctive relation to both things and persons is that of acquisition, power, we may instance the Babbitt of Sinclair Lewis, and Soames Forsyte of Galsworthy's *The Forsyte Saga*.

Throughout *Babbitt* there is suggestion—no more—of a personal tragedy. The narrow outlook, the banal speech, the muddled thinking, of Babbitt and his group are depicted remorselessly and at length; yet in the central figure, behind the character mask, are motions of a groping, dissatisfied spirit. Some glimpse of natural beauty, or, it might be, an impact of words that once had magic, waken in Babbitt feelings of disgust for his socially prescribed routine of money-making enterprise and convivial leisure. Yet a 'genius of authentic love', the author tells us, in Babbitt 'for his neighbourhood, his city, his clan', betrays this struggling other self. When his fellow-feeling is aroused for men on strike—the marching men that 'don't all look like such tough nuts. Look just about like anybody else to me'—his loyalty to his clan, the complete involvement of his life with his group, force on him abandonment of his faintly attempted revolt. The last words of the story echo the hint of tragedy, when Babbitt warns his son not to be so scared, 'the way I've been', of the family, of Zenith, of his own self.

In the story of Soames Forsyte, as told in *The Forsyte Saga* and *A Modern Comedy*, the tragic pattern of blind error and nemesis stands out more clearly. A reader accustomed to more economical styles of writing now current may feel tedium in the story's setting—the detail by help of which Galsworthy 'embalms' his Victorian middle-class family. But the story of Soames is poignant, as the author traces the fatality of the selfish possessive claim inflicted first by the husband upon the wife, then watched, in pain and understanding, by the father when, in his daughter, in relation to the man of her choice, the same instinct appears unbridled.

That appeal of beauty, which at times stirred Babbitt to revulsion against the routine of his life, affected Soames more powerfully. Felt in a glowing landscape, in the pictures he collected, in (most of all) the woman, Irene, beauty disturbed Soames; but the dominant Forsyte character—diagnosed by the most perceptive member of the clan as the sense of property and the inability to surrender oneself—transformed response to beauty into dogged impulse to possess. Tormented by the consciousness that, legal possession attained, the spirit of Irene, his wife, still escaped him, Soames is driven to assert his marital rights brutally and arouse in the woman lasting enmity. His penance is exacted through his relation to his daughter (by a second more utilitarian marriage). When first he sees his new-born baby, the sense of triumphant possession stirs, though beyond it is awareness of 'something individual, bud-like and touching'. Living into an age that has shattered the Forsyte

ideal of ownership in family relations, Soames learns a
different attitude.[1] To keep his daughter's affection he finds
he must endure and sacrifice much. As Galsworthy unfolds
his plot of the daughter pursuing, with the same dogged
impulse, the son of the woman the father had desired and
violated, Soames is shown learning at last something of the
meaning of love—love that is human and complete, with its
gift of insight into another's need and outlook, and light
thrown back upon oneself. When death comes to Soames,
still intent on care for his daughter, we feel that his penance,
accomplished, has brought what enlightenment his nature
could admit.

The necessary limitations of this essay forbid that I should
venture here to analyse, in however summary a fashion,
other works of fiction that present the theme of human
bondage and deliverance. If I might write at length of
novels that have made vivid to me the thought of a life-
discipline that can liberate in some degree the spirit 'fastened
to a dying animal', I would speak of the writings of H. G.
Wells, not as works of literary art but for their repeated
picturing of the painful struggle with instinctive craving,
sex-possessiveness, anger, jealousy, and of emergence, gradual
and partial, into freedom of a communion within which
science, art, history, have their being, and disinterested devotion becomes possible to these and to one's fellow-beings.

[1] Such a lesson, one recalls, could hardly have been learned in former times
by a parent of similar character. Christian beliefs could not teach it
when—as Virginia Woolf has reminded us, quoting from Trevelyan's
History of England—a disobedient daughter 'was liable to be locked up,
beaten and flung about the room without any shock being inflicted on
public opinion'; or when—as we read in Abbott's translations of the
monkish records of the miracles of St. Thomas of Canterbury—a thirteen-
year-old girl, 'daughter of a man of no mean rank', could be driven to
attempt suicide by her mother's cruel threats and beatings for a slight
offence—the story taken apparently, Abbott notes, from a sermon 'to
some village congregation in the neighbourhood'. The attitude of preacher
and monkish recorder—intent on the miracle of the girl's rescue from
death as a mercy by the saint's favour bestowed on the unworthy, without
comment on the behaviour of the mother—suggests a comparison, not to
our detriment, between spiritual vision in that 'age of faith' and our own,
as expr essed in terms of human relationship.

A novel of more literary charm than those of Wells, but again, for me, with another than aesthetic value, is *Howard's End* by E. M. Forster. Problems of personal relationship are vividly illustrated in the story of Margaret and Helen Schlegel and the family of the Wilcoxes. The figure of Margaret, through her part in the story and sometimes directly through her speech, conveys a distinctive idea concerning wisdom in personal relations—a wisdom requiring that the spirit should come to terms with the flesh and the world it creates 'of telegrams and anger'. 'Don't brood too much', Margaret tells her sister, 'on the superiority of the unseen to the seen. Our business is not to contrast the two but to reconcile them.'

For serious imaginative treatment of the theme of personal relationship, one need not, however, turn to books found memorable in former decades. In any year's output novels may be found that deal with aspects of the struggle towards relations more true and adequate. Among those concerned with the effort towards justice and fellowship between men of different race, I think of Alan Porter's novel, *Cry, the Beloved Country* (Cape, 1948). For me there is power and beauty in the image—conveyed indirectly through his influence upon others after death—of the white man who had given his life to the cause of justice between white and black in South Africa. What drove him into that service, his private papers recorded, was the conflict, felt in his own soul, between faith in human brotherhood and its denial in the established social order.

As illustrating this conflict between society's order, or disorder, and the felt needs of the human spirit, I choose to refer to the work of one other contemporary writer, John Steinbeck. His *Grapes of Wrath* is a powerful indictment of economic disorder, but I choose rather the slighter story, *The Moon is Down*, for the sake of a passage that I feel illumines with peculiar vividness the conflict between

spiritual insight—or one might say the Divine persuasion—
and an outward order that enslaves the will.

The Colonel Lanser of Steinbeck's story—commanding
the Nazi troops that occupied a nameless, isolated mining
town in a country we think of as Norway—is shown as a
man of some sensitiveness in personal relations. He has had
experience of war, and has learnt 'that war is treachery and
hatred . . . torture and killing and sickness and tiredness,
until at last it is over and nothing has changed except for
new weariness and new hatreds'; yet he tries to put aside
these sick memories and to carry out the orders he receives.
In his dealings with Orden, mayor of the little town, he
respects him as a man faithfully obedient to the democratic
order he represents. As the town's resistance develops, a
position is reached when Mayor Orden, as a hostage, must
be executed. Preparing his spirit for death, the mayor, in
talk with a friend, recalls words from the *Apology*, recited
once by him at a school graduation. As he repeats, with
hesitation, the words spoken by Socrates to the men who
have condemned him: how 'in the hour of death men are
gifted with prophetic power. And I—prophesy to you
who are my murderers—that immediately after my—my
death—', his friend substitutes the word 'departure'; and
Orden, seeing Colonel Lanser watching him, asks him for
the right word, and is prompted: ' "Departure". It is
"immediately after my departure".' 'Then Orden looked
straight ahead and his eyes were in his memory, seeing
nothing outward'; and as he continued that immortal indictment, 'after my departure punishment far heavier than
you have inflicted on me will surely await you', both his
friend and Colonel Lanser 'seemed to be trying to help
him to remember'. The mayor has still before him a possibility of saving his life by choosing to collaborate, but he
refuses, and the Colonel, though knowing they will fail,
carries out his orders.

M I

The passage, in its setting, has seemed to me an instance, as vivid as any I know in fiction, of the moment that may come to any man, when, in relation to another's spirit—to Jesus Christ perhaps, or Socrates, speaking in the present through another's mouth—he is addressed by the Eternal Wisdom, and listens—hearing a word, in conflict perhaps with all the habit of a lifetime—and either obeys or refuses.

This moment imagined by Steinbeck, of unavailing insight in a Nazi soldier, may remind us of a like unavailing enlightenment, through experience interpreted by the Presence that Arthur Koestler in *Darkness at Noon* has named the Silent Partner. Both these novels, telling of the enslavement of an individual will by a totalitarian régime using the resources of present-day psychological technique, may serve to illustrate the view that it is not so much alternation, as Sorokin argues, of spiritual and 'sensate' apprehension that characterizes the succession of the ages; but rather, as Reinhold Niebuhr has urged, the development of each form both for good and ill. The growing knowledge of its material and psychic medium that increases the insight and power of the spirit, increases also the power and range of unspiritual impulses, self- and group-centred, evil.

In these brief and varied references to recent imaginative writings, no image has appeared that could readily be compared with those found in ancient records, of sage, prophet, saint. The question of the relation of these illustrations to 'the type-image of wisdom' seems to require further discussion, which will be attempted in relation to the wider question regarding the meaning to be attached to the terms, 'type-image', 'archetype', and the significance in social and individual life of the realities for which these terms stand.

'The Zurich school', Jung has written, 'regards the fundamental thoughts and impulses of the unconscious as symbols
indicative of a definite line of future development.' He refers
here especially to development in the individual. Similarly
in the history of civilization 'the functional importance of
the symbol is clearly shown. . . . The further development
of mankind can only be brought about by means of
symbols which represent something far in advance of
himself and whose intellectual meaning cannot be grasped
entirely.'[1]

These sayings represent the aspect of Jung's thought
which I have attempted chiefly to illustrate in these
essays. The hypothesis which Jung's experience with
his patients appears to confirm, and which I have
found illumining in literary and historical study, assigns
to those 'fundamental thoughts and impulses' which
Jung terms 'archetypes' a two-fold aspect. The archetype
is both a product of time, the shape in which it
appears determined by past history, and also a creative
energy, looking towards and helping to determine
the future.

In characterizing one of these aspects Jung is not scrupu-
lous to keep in mind the other. Although when his general
attitude is in question he insists on the necessity of the final
point of view, the inadequacy of the purely causal standpoint, he is nevertheless frequently content to define the
archetype, or primordial image, by its relation to the past,
as a trace or deposit of racial experience. The reflective
reader who would grasp Jung's complete meaning must
understand these definitions in the light of Jung's faith in
the creative power of the mind exercised both in the

---

[1] From Author's Preface to First Edition of *Collected Papers on Analytical
Psychology* (translated by C. E. Long, London, 1917).

M2

formation during past ages, and in the present use, of the archetypal image.[1]

As an illustration of Jung's method we may refer to his discussion of the 'Wotan archetype', as a primordial image 'invading' the minds of the German people under Nazi rule. In the course of this discussion he generalizes: 'Archetypes are like river-beds which the water has abandoned, but to which it returns again after an indefinitely long period. An archetype is like the course of an old river in which the waters of life having flowed a long time have worn a deep channel. The longer they were contained in the same bed, the more likely are they sooner or later to return to it.'[2] The simile of the reflooded river-bed is arresting. In this instance it applies so well to the overwhelming of the conscious mind by fierce primitive impulses, of aggression, acquisition, racial antagonism, that had been latent, released and canalized by the image of the awakened war-god and his band of raging Nordic warriors. Yet the aptness of the simile hardly justifies the generalization: archetypes are like river-beds, abandoned water-courses. This is to ignore the dynamic aspect present if we survey the whole image of the reflooding water bringing possibilities of change[3] to an existing ancient configuration. From the Wotan image the creative aspect is not absent. Wotan, the ancient war-god, was also the god of runes, of poetry and

---

[1] See particularly his discussion of the creative power of the mind exercised in fashioning the myth of divine rebirth from the perceived movements of the sun and the seasonal changes. *Psychological Types* (London, 1923), pp. 556-7.

[2] From an article, 'Wotan', first published 1936. In English translation included in *Essays on Contemporary Events* (Kegan Paul, 1948).

[3] 'An atavism gripped me' says a Jewish writer (in *The New Statesman and Nation*, 2 July, 1949) describing the emotion experienced when participating in a ceremony of the Hassidim, 'a fossilized schism of mystics'. In the same paragraph he writes of their Messianic conviction 'swirling down secular channels' to make the State of Israel. An 'atavism' might be an alternative term for the archetype in its archaic aspect, but even as we name 'atavism' this force that grips living men, thought passes to its creative aspect, the social and political changes that, vehement like a torrent, it effects.

prophesy, the wisdom of those days. At times, and to some minds, in the recent history of Germany, there must have appeared the Messianic aspect of the Wotan archetype, and the image that presented itself was not of the savage warrior, but of the deliverer who, under conditions of civilized understanding between peoples, might lead his nation in new ways based on its heritage of science, art, philosophy.

In writing of man's 'search for a soul' Jung has described the archetypes as 'psychic organs', that may become 'atrophied', but whose right functioning is necessary to mental and spiritual health.[1] Such an organ would be the archetype of saving wisdom, appearing as the image of a deliverer, or guide, in time of need. 'The archetypal image of the wise man, the saviour or redeemer', Jung has written, 'is awakened whenever the times are out of joint', when 'conscious life is characterized by onesidedness'.[2]

Such an awakening may be in the experience of a nation or of an individual. Of the appearing to an individual of the type-image of the sage, an instance has been given from his medical practice by Dr. H. G. Baynes. He cites the case of a 'terribly one-sided' extraverted American doctor 'who told of an occasion when, having come home after an over-filled day, limp and dazed with exhaustion, he sat half-dozing in his surgery. In a kind of trance he saw, standing upon the table beside him, a little image . . . the figure of a mature man in a simple robe, carrying a staff in his right hand. As he described this figure my patient broke down and wept. He knew that this apparition, which he had seen standing in front of him as a simple image, was the real desire of his whole being.'[3]

The image in this instance bore outward resemblance to the Eastern sage who sought spiritual wisdom in a wandering life of meditation and ascetic poverty. Yet the individual,

[1] *Modern Man in Search of a Soul* (Kegan Paul, 8th impression, 1945), p. 130
[2] *ibid.*, p. 197.
[3] *Germany Possessed*, by H. G. Baynes (Cape, 1941), p. 167.

recognizing the image as a symbol of his own desire would stress the inward, universal, not the outward character of the ancient seeker after wisdom. It is this inward character that I have tried to illustrate in the present essay. Thinking of the archetype as a necessary organ or function of the human mind, one must look for the universal element in the image mainly in its relation to the mind that recognizes and responds. Only thus, I think, can we feel a common character in figures so diverse as those of the great teacher, or visionary, of the past, and, in the present, the great political leader, or the literary artist and the visions he presents.

Two contemporary novelists, in a recently published exchange of views,[1] considering their art in its relation to society, speak of the way a writer's work 'begins a life of its own after it leaves his hands'. 'By means of its writers', says V. S. Pritchett, 'a society communicates with itself.' In these words I find a rendering of my theme of the imaginative writer as making distinct and vivid for the responsive reader type-images already in his mind. Following the same line of thought, Miss Bowen speaks of being 'on the edge of a hazy idea that the artist, in these days, is being sought, focused on . . . because he seems to be a conferer of shape, an interpreter of direction'. There is sóme 'ordinary human modicum' of wisdom, or 'common sense', which 'appears in our writing because it appears in us; but because it is mixed with vision, or whatever else one calls imaginative perception, it sounds Delphic'. 'Delphic', like the voice of a god, the words of the literary artist sound when, 'mixed with vision', they render back to us our own truth, a wisdom which the course of events impinging on our spirits, has already obscurely taught.

At a recitation of Homer, the auditor, Plato declared,

---

[1] *Why do I Write? An Exchange of Views between Elizabeth Bowen, Graham Greene, V. S. Pritchett* (London, 1948).

was the last link of a chain, as it were magnetized by a common inspiration, the Muse communicating through those whom she has first inspired an influence to all capable of sharing it.[1] The imaginative writer of to-day, whether poet or novelist, seems, like the ancient bard, to write not altogether from his individual thought and feeling, but rather to be the spokesman of thoughts generated through the act of communication—his deeper mind in communion with other minds of his time.

It is in accordance with this view of the relation between the novelist and his time that we find depicted by the novelist of to-day no figure embodying in any satisfying degree an ideal of wisdom. The thought and belief of our age is too complex, too divided, to generate such an image. If, through our own spirit's need we seek it, we find no more than hints of the direction in which true wisdom lies. In the few novels of which I have spoken, and in many others, we find indications of a direction of spiritual growth, away from the self-centred blindness of the man of property, the man of violence, towards no final vision but a communion with others that opens many differing, partial perspectives of ultimate divine truth.

Water reflooding an abandoned river-bed; a psychic organ atrophied or functioning; a common impulse operating—or common inspiration by the muse's grace flowing—between the minds of author and reader: such descriptions may at times excite in us a vexed impatience. Can we not speak more plainly? Can we not show some clear concept, or frame of thought, underlying this rush of metaphorical description and varied illustration?

Some feeling such as this perhaps operates, and is appeased, when we speak, with Jung, of brain paths. The primordial image, or archetype, Jung writes, 'is the psychic

[1] *Ion; or, of the Iliad.*

expression of an anatomically or physiologically determined disposition'.[1] The reference to physiological dispositions seems to take us into the sphere of science, of spatial, material structures, away from the region where feelings and impulses and imagined forms melt into one another like colours in moving water.

Yet it seems to me that we gain little by reference to the material brain when we necessarily approach our subject not as spatial happenings within the skull, but in the form of thoughts, feelings, impulses, finding expression in speech and personal behaviour. However we shape our hypotheses concerning the psychic forces operative within this speech and action, we can make reference to a supposed brain structure determining the psychic functioning. Such reference helps little unless or until experimental verification is possible. The reference in Jung's case seems to me to have little, if any, influence on his account of what he has learnt from contact with his patients, and reflection on his own experience—an account that subordinates constantly any aim at scientific exactness to the need to follow freely those hints and suggestions so fascinating to any student in intimate contact with minds and their products.

Dr. E. B. Strauss has commented on the method of psychologists, especially of those producing theories in the sphere of medical or dynamic psychology. For the purposes of his study, the psychologist, says Dr. Strauss, abstracts from 'the psycho-physical unit called man' something he perhaps terms an instinct. He can then 'go ahead and discern the presence and working-out of this instinct in man's every act, thought and feeling'. He can 'do this correctly since there is no truly watertight compartment in the psychic life of man'. The theoretic construction he thus elaborates may be 'impressive and valuable', and can only be properly criticized within its own framework and terms,

[1] *Psychological Types*, p. 556.

but should not be used to deny and depreciate all other psychologies'.[1]

This account of method, which seems to me an apt comment on the work of the Freudian school, I accept as also applicable to the writings of Jung, and to my own study of the pervasive influence of archetypes in mental process. It is that character of psychic life which Dr. Strauss describes as having no watertight compartment that gives such seductive freedom to one following the track of some element or impulse discerned as significant in imaginative and religious experience.[2] It is the same character that Bergson describes as interpenetration, the qualities and moments of 'real duration' permeating one another, in contrast with the mutually external, spatialized characters of conceptual time, and of scientific and logical concepts. The intellect, adapted to dealing with the material and spatial, is adapted ill, Bergson notes, to the study of the psychic, the non-spatial.

Yet we cannot, in studying this baffling, alluring, inter-penetrative psychic life, abandon the effort of the intellect to define, or make as distinct as possible, the meaning of the terms we use. If we consider again the elusive term, 'archetype', as used by Jung, and as accepted from him by some recent writers, we can distinguish, I think, certain aspects of meaning that recur with varying emphasis.

The term, 'archetype', may refer mainly to tendencies within the body-mind, such as academic psychologists have named psycho-physical dispositions;[3] or it may refer

---

[1] Address from the Chair to the medical section of the British Psychological Society, January, 1946. Printed in the *Brit. J. of Med. Psychol.* Vol. XXI, Part I.

[2] The psychologist admiring the ready compliance of his psychic material with his chosen plan of exposition, can say, with Bunyan reflecting on his own use of the type-image of the pilgrim: 'having now my method by the end,
      Still as I pulled, it came'.

[3] By this term psychologists left open the vexed question of the relation of mind and body, keeping the reference to the body while their study was of mental happenings.

more particularly to images handed down from one
generation to another, and preserved in books and
pictures. When Jung speaks of 'psychic organs', it is the
disposition, the subjective factor that he has in mind.
But when he names, for instance, 'the Wotan archetype',
it is of the more objective factor he is thinking. Here
he can follow the cultural history of the archetypal image
as tradition presents it in pictorial shapes and language
symbols.

When Jung's concept of the archetype is adopted by the
sociologist it is the objective, traditional image whose
appearances he studies in social life, while keeping in view
also the subjective aspect, the emotional response that gives
value to the image. When Professor Mannheim writes of
'Christian archetypes', he is concerned directly with the
'concrete image containing the whole historical and social
setting in which it occurred', and requiring, when conditions change, a re-interpretation 'to adapt the meaning
of the archetype to the new situation'.[1]

In addition to Jung's term 'archetype' or 'primordial
image', we might use, Dr. Mannheim has suggested, to
denote the individual's response, the term 'paradigmatic'
experience—for which rather repellent coinage Dr. Oldham
has proposed the term 'commanding' experience.[2] By such
archetypal images as the sage, the saint, the saviour, when
in men's daily life they continuously appeared—expressed
in current speech, literature, ceremony—commanding experiences were awakened and maintained that could direct
the thought and life of men in society. When such images
no longer operate, Mannheim urges, social life becomes
disintegrated, 'despiritualized'. It is the same thought
applied in relation to society that Jung expresses in relation
to the individual, when he speaks of a psychic organ that

[1] *Diagnosis of Our Time* (Kegan Paul, 1943), p. 118.
[2] In *The Christian News-Letter Supplement*, 24 February 1943.

becomes atrophied when the individual no longer reverences any image of the Divine.

My own study of archetypes I have expressed in terms of 'type-images', present in imaginative and religious writings, and of 'needs' corresponding to these, felt or latent in individual minds. I also have found the question arise which Mannheim considers, as to the effect in present-day social life of the decreasing emphasis upon those type-images which the Christian teaching of their day brought home to the minds of our forefathers.

The question has far-reaching issues that could not be considered in this essay; but in the line of thought I have followed there is an implication I should like, in this review of the discussion, to make more explicit. I have argued that the individual to-day who cannot accept completely the teaching of the Christian churches may yet in his encounter through literature with thinkers past and present, or in personal relation with present-day leaders and friends, so realize the archetypes of saving wisdom and of spiritual rebirth as to share in the religious life and fellowship that to others has been mediated by the Christian churches, or the great religions of the East. In so arguing I have not thought of this realization of the archetype as a meeting simply of subjective human need and objective traditional image. I have assumed, with Jung, that the individual mind brings to the encounter a creative activity, and that creative activity went to the fashioning of the image in the past. But also, I have believed that in the encounter there is co-operation of an influence, termed by the philosopher Whitehead, the Divine persuasion, and, by theologians, the Grace of God.

When the archetype of saving wisdom appears to me, a living being, in the form of another living person, the psychologist may speak of the projection of an image; but it is not in this way that I naturally think of the encounter.

I realize it as a meeting of one incarnate spirit directly with another. Even so direct may appear the spiritual meeting that in historic time has been mediated by an earlier encounter and its record; such as that between Socrates and Plato, or between the Christ-spirit and St. Paul or the author of the Fourth Gospel. In such encounter, either, through records, with the great spirits of the past, or through personal relation with the living, I know the mystery of the Divine life and wisdom transmitted to me through finite beings.[1] In Buber's language, the Eternal is encountered through the finite *Thou.*

At this point, conceiving the relation of the archetype of saving wisdom to the Divine Mind, we may think of the use by St. Thomas Aquinas of the term 'archetype' or 'prototypal form'. Of prototypes in the Divine Mind St. Thomas says: 'they are really not other than the divine essence according as its similitude can be participated in by divers things in divers ways'.[2] Is there a relation between the archetype of saving wisdom considered in this essay, and the ancient thought of a prototype, or many prototypal

---

[1] Such a momentous meeting may be with a friend after death whose spirit seems to enter the life that had been devastated by loss, as a rebirth of energy for living, perhaps as an assurance even beyond the limits of this life. A poem by C. Day Lewis has described, as perfectly as words may, this experience, telling how the dead friend 'sprang to life again':

He bore transplanting
Into a common soil. Strongly he grows
  Upon the heart and gives the tentative wing
Take-off for flights, surety for repose.
. . . . through
Desert my heart he gives a fiery lead
Unfolding contours, lengthening the view.
He is a thoroughfare
Over all sliding sands. Each stopping place
Wears his look of welcome. May even find,
When I come to the snow-line, the bitter end,
His hand-holds cut on death's terrific face.

(From 'A Time to Dance' in *Collected Poems, 1929-1936.*
Hogarth Press, 1948.)

[2] From *Summa Theologica*, as quoted by Dr. Emmet, comparing the passage with Whitehead's view, in *Whitehead's Philosophy of Organism* (Macmillan, 1932), p. 120.

forms in the mind of God, in accordance with which he fashioned the world and man?

We need not for our present purpose ask how, in relation to his whole system, St. Thomas thought of prototypes. We consider, rather, the notion that has haunted the minds of many religious thinkers—and of which the statement quoted offers one expression—of an ideal that is for each man the divine intention; and for an answer to our question, concerning the relation to this of the archetype of wisdom, may find suggestion in the writings both of Whitehead, and of Jung when he ventures beyond his usual psychological standpoint.

At the end of his essay on 'The Relation between the Ego and the Unconscious',[1] Jung discusses what he terms a transcendental postulate, or hypothesis, of a self that can be 'the goal of life, because it is the most complete expression of that fateful combination we call individuality'. This self is to the conscious ego as the sun to the earth. It includes the sum of those unconscious contents which can 'become manifest in their capacity to thwart the will, to obsess consciousness'. It can be called 'the god in us', though it contains forces that, repressed and distorted, forcing their way into action, may appear devilish.

If we accept from Jung the hypothesis of such an inclusive self, which, as a 'goal of individuation', would be what each of us might become if all our latent possibilites could be harmoniously fulfilled, would this self correspond to that archetype indicated in St. Thomas's words: 'not other than the divine essence according as its similitude can be participated in by divers [men] in divers ways'?

In his book, *Adventures of Ideas*,[2] Whitehead has developed his thought of the divine persuasion, illustrating it chiefly

[1] In *Two Essays on Analytical Psychology*, translated W. G. and C. F. Baynes (London, 1928), pp. 265-268.
[2] Part I, Chapter II: *The Human Soul*.

by reference to the Idea of 'the intellectual and moral grandeur of the human soul'. This ideal, he says, haunted the ancient Mediterranean world. It found one 'special expression' in the writings of Plato, another in the teaching of Jesus and the New Testament writers. It operated as a hidden force undermining institutions such as slavery, incompatible with it though at first accepted, even by those who preached the ideal, as inevitable. It was embodied partially and gradually through many specialized reforms. To its haunting presence sceptical humanitarians and fervent Quakers and Methodists responded, preaching it each in his distinctive terms.

In this survey of the influence of the idea of human worth, Whitehead emphasizes the social and universal aspect of that archetype of the fulfilled self—the divine intention for man—of which Jung speaks in relation to the individual. For man, a social being, there can be no final satisfaction apart from relation to his fellows; yet there often appears difference, even incompatibility, between the universal aspect of the ideal and that pursuit of individual fulfilment suggested by Jung. The individual called to the service of his fellows may sacrifice much that seemed necessary to his own fulfilment; while one seeking self-fulfilment will sacrifice possibilities of service.

'God has made out of his abundance a separate wisdom for every creature, and to do these things is my wisdom'. Of this saying I cannot trace the source, though I find it associated in my mind with William Morris, and the 'things' it was his wisdom to do; his beloved craftwork and writings and—when he felt in his distinctive manner the universal aspect of his own need—his uncongenial labours in the cause of socialism. Each of us perhaps has known moments, of effort or achievement, in communion with a loved person or with the great spirits of the past, when we seemed to know the end we were made for, the part

assigned us in the divine wisdom. Can we trust such
moments?

> Now God be thanked who has matched us with his hour,
> And caught our youth, and wakened us from sleeping.

Caught into the opening phases of a disastrous war, Rupert
Brooke, for the time when he wrote his 1914 sonnets, seemed
to know release and rebirth and fulfilment. Yet, we think,
he was mistaken. The fulfilment he experienced, in
surrender to a greater whole of the known self of the past,
was such as German soldiers also experienced, submerged
in the flooding of those forces Jung has named the Wotan
archetype.[1]

Among those possibilities of our nature whose harmonious
fulfilment would be the wisdom made by God for us are
many whose emergence into conscious activity brings
disaster, clashing with other possibilities seen later to be of
higher worth. Those of us who have faith in a Divine
wisdom that persuades toward harmony know how resistant
are those physical agencies whose co-operation is necessary
for all earthly attainment. Conflicting tendencies established
within our own nature obscure and distort the spirit's
insight, so that evil may follow decisions made in moments
of highest assurance.

We who cannot believe in an omnipotent God, nor in a
uniquely divine revelation, must do without certainty, without safety—with whatever completeness of personal adhesion

---

[1] In an interesting discussion in his book, *The Poetry of W. B. Yeats* (Oxford
University Press, 1941) of the nature of our present revulsion against the
emotion expressed in these sonnets by Rupert Brooke, Louis MacNeice
has condemned them as false to life, lacking 'profound natural sanction',
and thus illusory in a manner in which an impassioned love-poem is not
illusory. The distinction cannot, I think, be maintained. Ecstasy in
surrender of the individual to the national or tribal will, like the surrender
to sex-love, is an emotion so deeply based as to have 'profound natural
sanction' as a theme for poetry. Yet we may attribute higher value to such
poetry as that of Wilfred Owen, where the instinctive emotion released by
war has given place to the more mature emotion of pity.

we hold our faith. Yet this much our faith gives us: accepting in relation to our own lives what image-symbols to us best represent Divine birth into the human condition, Divine wisdom in human limitation, we cannot find our individual life lacking in meaning, nor the world of our experience despiritualized.

INDEX

I.—SUBJECTS

*Subjects sufficiently indicated in the Analytical Table of
Contents (pp. vii-xii) are not included.*

Age, aged, 52, 110f, 118
Apocalyptic literature, 80
Archetype -s, 9, 21f, 27, 59, 104, 126,
    131, 166ff, 173ff
— of the fulfilled self, 177f
— of God transcendent, 10, 34f
— of Heaven, 57
— of numinous birth, 64, 87f, 93
— of rebirth, 11, 158, 175
— of saving wisdom, 166, 175f
— of the suffering god, hero,
    servant, 10, 34, 83f
Art, 105, 111, 140
Aryan religion, 71, 80

Body (in contrast with spirit), 15, 32,
    50, 53, 91, 103, 111, 160
Buddhism, 77, 119, 122

Child (as a symbol), 89f
Christ (of inner experience), 11, 27,
    36, 114f, 176
Christian church -es, 85, 128ff, 147,
    153, 175
— ethics, 92
— religion, worship, 3, 8, 21, 160
Clay (as a symbol), 107
Cradle (as a symbol), 68f, 91

Death, 52, 55ff, 96ff, 108, 123f, 132
Devil, Devilish, 19, 23, 32, 58, 108
Divine intention, 23, 42, 45, 177f
— Kingdom, 80f, 85, 90
— persuasion, 37, 41, 165, 175,
    177
— vision, 19f, 36, 49f, 55f
Dual code, 142f

Ecstacy, 17, 71f
Encounter, with the Divine, 1, 15,
    17, 24, 46, 60f, 102f, 115, 156
Entry, of the Divine, 64, 74, 86, 105f
Emancipation, 117ff
Eternal, Eternity, 37, 61, 106, 111,
    125, 155f, 166, 176

Evil, 21, 33ff, 65, 72, 78f, 90f, 96,
    106ff, 157, 166, 179
Existentialist, 151

Faith, in God, 1f, 21, 32, 34, 46, 51f,
    58, 74, 106, 180

Golden age, 90f
Grace of God, 32, 48, 50, 175
Guilt, 30, 34, 39

Hell, 7f, 157
Historic studies, history, 41f, 80, 84,
    106, 115f, 167

Immortality, 52f, 71, 119
I-Thou relation, 1, 24f, 33f, 41, 43,
    69, 119, 160

King, as type-figure, kingship, 126,
    134, 136ff

Logos, 113, 116, 141, 143
Love, creative, 89, 163

Magic, 82, 96, 130, 138
Mystery, 85, 103, 108, 132ff, 152,
    158, 176
— religion, 11f, 114
Myth, 6, 49, 57, 68, 75f, 150, 158f
— of divine conflict, 78ff

Nirvana, 117f, 141
Numinous personality, 119, 121

Order, right, 136f, 140f, 149
— types of, 35, 51

Philosopher, philosophy, 5, 20, 24f,
    27, 51, 106, 150f
Poetry, 73, 95, 103ff, 124, 138, 142,
    150, 156ff
Political action, politics, 40f, 151
Prayer, 47ff, 101, 110f, 113
Priestly tradition, 127ff
Psychology, 9, 11, 31, 124, 172

Reason, 23f, 32, 37, 49, 59, 108, 114
Ritual pattern, 12, 68

Sacrifice, 12, 15f, 83f, 126ff, 132
Science, 14, 22, 59, 84, 147, 172
Serpent, 79, 106f
Sociologist, 22, 110, 112, 155, 174
Son of man, 80ff, 86

Sphinx-image, 93
Symbolism, symbols, 27, 108

Truth, divine, 5, 55, 171
— human, 8, 60, 74, 98, 104f, 115, 117, 122, 125, 157, 170
Tragedy, 106, 134, 138, 161f

Wotan archetype, 168f, 174, 179

II—NAMES

(AUTHORS' AND OTHERS)

Abbot, E., 132, 163n
Æ, 72
Aeschylus, 159
Andrewes, Bishop, 97
Andrews, C. F., 86
Aquinas, Thomas, 148, 176
Arthur, King, 139ff
Asoka, 120f, 128
Auden, W. H., 50, 99

Bacon, B. W., 12
Baillie, John, 2, 24
Baynes, H. G., 107n, 169
Becket, Thomas, 127ff
Benda, Julien, 148ff
Berdaev, 49n
Bergson, 173
Blok, A., 87n
Bowen, E., 170
Bowra, C. M., 87n
Brooke, Rupert, 179
Browning, Robert, 101
Buber, Martin, 1, 24f, 33, 43, 160
Buddha, see Gautama
Bunyan, 173n
Burns, Delisle, 130f

Churchill, Winston, 144, 146
Collingwood, R. G., 140
Confucius, 149
Coomaraswamy, A. K., 74n
Cornford, F. M., 10, 17

Dante, 19, 100, 157
Dark, Sidney, 129n
Davids, T. W. Rhys, 117ff, 128
Dawson, C., 125f, 135, 137, 149
Durkheim, 11

Eisler, 71
Elgar, 56
Eliot, T. S., 49, 96, 132ff, 156f
Elwes, Gervase, 57
Emmet, D. M., 176n
Empedocles, 70
Erasmus, 148, 150
Euripides, 72

Frankfort, H., 136
orster, E. M., 164

Galsworthy, J., 161ff
Gandhi, 75, 85f
Gasset, Ortega, 20
Gautama, Buddha, 77f, 146ff, 127
George, Stefan, 87n
Gladstone, 39
Goethe, 149, 150f

Hammond, J. L., 39
Harrison, Jane, 2ff, 13f, 68
Henry II, 129ff, 134
Hesiod, 20, 112, 139, 144
Hitler, 18
Hooke, S. H., 84
Housman, A. E., 53
Huxley, Aldous, 21, 40f, 75n
Huxley, Julian, 44n, 46

Isherwood, C., 50, 75n

James, E. O., 12
Jaspers, K., 58f
Jesus (the historic), 8, 10, 26, 28, 77f,
    81ff, 89f, 113ff, 142, 154, 178
John, St., 11, 14
John of Salisbury, 131
Jung, C. G., 9, 107n, 123f, 167ff,
    171ff, 177ff

Kant, 150f
Keats, 142f
Keith, Arthur, 142f
Kennedy, H. A. A., 12
Keynes, J. M., 144f, 152
Kipling, 18
Koestler, Arthur, 22, 31, 60, 159, 166

Lattey, C., 48
Lenin, 18n
Lewis, Sinclair, 161
Lewis, C. Day, 176n
Lilienthal, D. E., 42ff
Lü Yen, 123f

MacNeice, L., 179n
Macmurray, J., 31
MacWilliams, C., 43n
Mannheim, K., 22, 174f
Marcell, Gabriel, 132f, 152
Marlowe, 138
Maynard, J., 18n

Maritain, J., 48
Maughan, Somerset, 54
Maximus of Tyre, 27
Mill, J. S., 112n
Milton, 73, 86, 95f, 99
Morris, William, 178
Murray, Gilbert, 18n

Newman, J. H., 56
Neill, Bishop, 96
Niebuhr, Reinhold, 49n, 166
Nietzsche, 87ff, 98

Oesterley, W. O. E., 79
Oldham, J. H., 22n, 174
Orr, J. Boyd, 46n
Otto, R., 64, 71, 78, 80ff, 121n

Paul, St., 11, 26, 89f, 114, 176
Pindar, 70
Plato, 5ff, 19, 26, 35ff, 55, 57, 103ff,
    150, 170, 176, 178
Porter, Alan, 164
Powys, Cowper, 52
Pritchett, V. S., 170

Radhakrishnan, 77n
Raine, K., 157, 159n
Rodhe, 71
Rousseau, 98

Saint-Exupéry, 15f, 60
Schweitzer, A., 8, 29ff, 32f
Shakespeare, 94, 138

Shelley, 67
Sierra, 27
Socrates, 103, 165f, 176
Sorokin, P. A., 112, 155f
Solomon, 139
Spender, S., 52n
Steinbeck, J., 43n, 164f
Strauss, E. B., 172f
Strong, L. A. G., 108n

Thompson, E., 121f
Tyrrell, G., 4

Virgil, 69, 100f, 140f

Wadia, A. R., 53n
Waley, A., 123n
Weber, A., 94
Wells, H. G., 165
Whitehead, A. N., 7, 35ff, 41, 107,
    124, 177
Wilhelm, 123n
Williams, Charles, 140ff
Williams, H., 145n
Wilson, Woodrow, 144ff
Wodehouse, H., 47f
Woolf, L., 145
Woolf, V., 163n
Wordsworth, William, 103ff

Yeats, W. B., 63ff, 87, 91, 93, 101f,
    106ff, 110f, 116, 124f

Zoroaster, 82